How To Study The Sacred

An Introduction to Religious Studies

Also available from the MSAC Philosophy Group

Spooky Physics

Darwin's DNA

The Magic of Consciousness

The Gnostic Mystery

When Scholars Study the Sacred

Mystics of India

The Unknowing Sage

String Theory

In Search of the Perfect Coke

Is the Universe an App?

Adventures in Science

You are Probability

The Mystical

Digital Philosophy

How To Study The Sacred

An Introduction to Religious Studies

Mt. San Antonio College
Walnut, California

Second Edition: 2014

ISBN: 978-1-56543-872-9

MSAC Philosophy Group
Mt. San Antonio College
1100 Walnut, California 91789 USA

Website: http://www.neuralsurfer.com

Imprint: *The Runnebohm Library Series*

Publication History: This book was first published in the United States as *Scholars Who Study the Sacred*. It was completed during Dr. Andrea Diem-Lane's sabbatical at Mt. San Antonio College during the latter part of the 1990s.

Dedication

To my husband, David Lane, and our two sons,
Shaun-Michael and Kelly-Joseph

Table of Contents

Introduction

There is an eastern parable about three blind men who visit an elephant and return to their home villages to describe this strange creature. One reported that an elephant is like a flat pancake since all he felt were the ears. Another described the animal as a long, fat snake since all he felt was the truck. And the third blind man characterized it as a big, round rock since all he felt was the body. While each description was correct in some way, all three were also limited. This classic story is rich with religious meaning. First of all, it symbolizes how religions may grasp some aspect of the Divine, yet fall short of a complete understanding. How could one comprehend the Infinite if it truly is infinite? The story also indicates that we can learn a great deal from each other. No matter how much we think we know, other traditions may add a new, necessary ingredient.

The lessons learned here apply to the academic study of religion as well. There are different scholarly perspectives on religion, from Marx to Weber to Freud to Jung to Durkheim, and each one, while at times in radical opposition, offers a valuable insight into religion. For instance, Marx's claim that religion maintains the status quo appears to be challenged by Weber's insistence that religion stimulates social change. Yet, based on the particular context in which they speak, both scholars may have captured a certain aspect of religion. For a well-rounded understanding of this subject it is important to entertain all of the diverse positions. Why do we find historians, psychologists, sociologists, anthropologists, even neurologists so interested in religion in the first place? Perhaps it is because religion is less about God than it is about human beings--representing our psycho-social-emotional-biological state, our cultural values, and our overall history.

The purpose of this book is to introduce the student to the main questions in Religious Studies and to survey some of the dominant theories drawing from a variety of disciplines. In Chapter One the question that concerns us is what religion is. Though this may seem like a straightforward type query we shall find out that there is much more involved. Religion cannot be defined so easily as several different definitions will be examined. Another important question, the topic of Chapter

Two, is where did religion come from. The origin of religion has always received as great deal of interest, for comprehending this gives us a handle on religion's overall purpose. Chapter Three focuses on why we should study religion to begin with. As expected from one with a degree in the subject, I shall argue that Religious Studies is one of the most important topics we can study for several reasons, but mainly because understanding another's philosophy in part determines our human relations. And, perhaps most importantly, the topic of methodology (how we should study religion) receives our attention in Chapter Four. The difference between Theology and Religious Studies and the value of Sociology of Religion and Transpersonal Psychology will be explained in this section. The last two chapters deal with the function of religion (what is its purpose) and the future of religion (where is religion heading).

Overall, this book is ideal for the introduction portion of a world religions course. Before jumping into the various belief systems and their histories it is important to explain the general dynamics of religion. Then when the student comes across Buddhist myths, Christian hagiography, Islamic ideological work, Hindu rituals, etc., one will be able to categorize it as such. Hopefully, at least in our understanding of religion, we need not remain as helplessly myopic as the blind men describing the elephant.

What is Religion?

Having attended Catholic school from first grade to my senior year in high school, I was taught that religion was defined as having a relationship with God. And this God was defined in very specific terms: a fatherly type figure who created the world and who oversees all actions. Though spiritually minded throughout my childhood, this notion of God always baffled me. I thought if God created everything, where then did God come from. At times I felt my brain would burst trying to comprehend this. I remember my first confessional in second grade where I nervously revealed to Father O'Connor my desire but incapability to grasp the truth of God. Expecting a revelation of some kind, an unveiling of the mysteries of the universe, I felt a bit shortchanged when he offered the Baltimore Catechism definition: God is the Holy Trinity. I would have been much more impressed if he quoted the ideas of Nicholas of Cusa who suggested that "The Unattainable is attained through Its unattainment." In other words, my not being able to grasp God was a good thing, for it meant that Reality was infinitely far greater than I could ever comprehend (although that may have been a bit too abstract for an eight-year old to understand). Perhaps detecting my disappointment or signs of early dissent the priest suggested that I meet him on the playground for further discussion. Not willing to reveal my identity, the philosophical discourse with the Irish priest never transpired. It was not until my first world religion course at the University of California that I confronted an entirely different view of religion and of God. Here I learned that, contrary to popular understanding, religion does not require a relationship with God or even a belief in a personal deity. In fact, there are many religions that are atheistic, such as certain Buddhist, Jain and Taoist schools. Moreover, for those religions that do profess a belief in God how one defines it is very idiosyncratic and can range from pantheism, to panentheism, to henotheism, to monism, to the view of God as female. So if the belief in God is not a prerequisite for religion, what then is? In this chapter we will investigate the classic definitions of religion as espoused by scholars in the field of Religious Studies.

The Latin word *religio* simply means to bind. But to bind with what? God? Nature? The Self? Perhaps the best way to put it is religion binds us with a sense of the sacred, whatever that may be. For Judeo-Christians the sacred is often depicted as an anthropomorphic being, God the Father. For Vedanta Hindus the sacred is a transcendental, impersonal, ineffable Reality, Brahman. And for Taoist the sacred is the harmony or balance of Nature. According to Mircea Eliade the sacred only can be understood in contrast to the profane [1]. For me the computer I am now working on falls under the profane category, for rarely, if ever, does it invoke a sense of something transcendental. Yet, with the scent of incense in the air and melodic chanting from Benedictine or Buddhist monks playing I am enthralled into a world of the numinous (derived from the Latin word numen meaning spirit), of feeling that there is something greater than myself and greater than all comprehension. This sense of awe, mystery and fascination was described by the German philosopher of religion Rudolf Otto as an "experience of the Wholly Other. [2]" Now I do not know whether this participation with the numinous is hard wired into my brain for evolutionary reasons (perhaps to supply me with some kind meaning so as to survive my existential states of mind and, as we know to be the goal of Nature, to pass on my DNA) or whether there is a mystical reality that transcends (and maybe includes) this material universe. On this subject, I claim Socratic ignorance as I openly admit my agnosticism [3].

Some philosophers make an interesting argument that the *world of matter is itself sacred* when understood from an Einsteinian perspective. Matter is not simply gray and flat but multi-layered and magnificent: from subatomic particles moving at the speed of light, to atoms, to molecules, to cells, to organisms, to ecosystems, to planets, to solar systems, to galaxies, to universes, to infinity. In fact, one confronts infinity at both the subatomic level which is forever divisible and the cosmic level which is ultimately uncontainable. When reflecting upon matter one can become awestruck. Richard Dawkins, a well-known scientist from Oxford University, captures this when he writes: "The feeling of awed wonder that science can give us is one of the highest experiences of which the human psyche is capable. It is a deep aesthetic passion to rank with the finest that music and poetry can deliver [4]." Einstein agreed that science can actually induce a feeling of mysteriousness and a sense of a connectedness with nature, and that is why this materialist atheist described himself as "belonging to the ranks of the most devoutly religious men.[5]" So can one be a materialist and be religious? The obvious answer is yes.

The theologian Paul Tillich slightly deviates from Eliade's definition of religion. According to Tillich, religion can be understood as one's "ultimate concern." Many have criticized this definition as being too nebulous and too inclusive. It seems to allow anything to be defined as a religion. Is surfing to Kelly Slater a religion? Indeed, I have had a few mystical visions myself surfing the blue waters of Hawaii. Is pursuing par game for golfers a religion? Well, certainly it's a contender. There is an indescribable high experienced when birdying a hole or sinking a thirty-foot putt. But I don't think Tillich had surfing and golfing in mind when he gave his definition. Rather, he meant that religion uniquely offers a sense of an "ultimate meaning" to one's life and a sense of transformation.

In defining religion, it is important to clarify what religion is not. W.C. Smith argues that religion must be understood as a "cumulative tradition," that is, as having gone through evolutionary stages, and not as a non-evolving "ism." To think of religion as static one has missed the dynamic nature and complexity of it. Hence, there is no such thing as Buddhism, Hinduism, Judaism, etc. Rather, there are Buddhist traditions, Hindu traditions, Jewish traditions, that have gone through numerous changes in history. For instance, in the Buddhist traditions there are Mahayana Buddhists including the schools of Zen, Pure Land, Tibetan, Nichiren Shoshu, etc., and Theravadist Buddhists. And all of these divisions promote teachings that may not have necessarily been from the mouth of the historical Buddha. Mahayana's reference to gods is a case in point, since Buddha appeared to have taught a more atheistic philosophy. The Hindu traditions are no exception, finding in its myriad followers of particular gods such as Shiva and Vishnu (there are 330 million gods according to the last count) and non-theists who acknowledge a higher impersonal reality, Brahman. In the Jewish traditions there are Conservative Jews, Orthodox Jews, Reformed Jews, Hasidic Jews, Kabalistic Jews, etc. Now to eliminate from our vocabulary any reference to religious isms would probably take a great deal of effort; somehow it is so much easier to say Judaism than the Jewish traditions. And I do not think that a crime has been committed if the ism word slips out or is part of our diction, as long as we remember that religions are complex and cumulative.

Classic Definitions of Religion

Eliade: Religion is an experience of the "sacred."

Otto: Religion is an experience of the "Wholly Other."

Tillich: Religion is one's "ultimate concern."

Smith: Religion is a "cumulative tradition" – not an "ism."

Smart: Religion is "a seven dimensional organism."

Perhaps the most popular definition of religion among scholars today comes from Ninian Smart [6]. He defines religion as an "organism with seven dimensions [7]." By organism Smart simply means that religion is alive and active, an idea that reiterates Smith's. The seven dimensions of this organism are the characteristics that make up a religion. These are: myths, rituals, religious experiences, doctrines, ethics, social institutions, and material forms of the religion. Smart contends that for a group to be defined as a religion it must possess all of these. Let us briefly look at what each dimension entails.

The Seven Dimensions of Religion

Myths: Sacred stories of two kinds: 1) historical myths filled with hagiography and symbolism and 2) purely symbolic myths

Rituals: Activities (usually repeated) that connect one with the sense of the sacred

Experiences: Religious experiences of the sacred; a feeling of the numinous

Doctrines: The philosophy or belief system of the religion

Ethics: The moral codes of the group

Social Aspect: The organizational form of the religion

Material Forms: The sacred objects of the religion

The Mythological Dimension

Myths, a term in Religious Studies not to be confused with false accounts, refer to stories about the sacred. These stories may have some historical backbone intermixed with a great deal of symbolism and hagiography (embellished accounts) or they may be purely symbolic. In order for a myth to be given historical status, the account must be falsifiable (able to be tested). Claims like god exists and god created so and so are non-testable and thus historically and scientifically meaningless.

An example of a historical type myth is birth of the Buddha. That he was actually born and that his parents were of royalty caste is viable. Yet, the claim that when the newborn entered the world he took seven steps and spoke words of wisdom, and that the earth shook and lotus flowers fell from the sky, is indeed dubious. It is a story to illustrate the Buddha's spiritual gifts and universe's rejoicing in them. The same critical analysis applies to the myth of Jesus. The assertion that there existed a religious teacher named Jesus (more correctly pronounced Yehoshu'a) has historical merit, since it is testable and has been tenuously verified by a couple of reports outside of the New Testament (to rely solely of the New Testament would not be good scholarship since its objectivity certainly remains questionable). Yet, there are several events of his life, including his birth, that are from an academic viewpoint laced with symbolism and hagiography. The virginal conception, indicating the purity of Jesus, is an illustration.

Why does embellishment of historical myths occur in the first place? The answer is simple: usually out of adoration for the subject (e.g., Jesus is so special he can walk on water) or to explain away a discrepancy (e.g., Jesus was born out of wedlock). The latter is referred to as "ideological work," an attempt to rationalize a contradiction between theology and praxis. In other words, when there is an inconsistency between one's theology and what has actually occurred there usually will be a great deal of effort to justify it. As an example, a guru, who is suppose to embody compassion and to have transcended worldly desires, may hit a disciple out of anger or sexually assault him or her[8]. Yet, instead of owning up to the abuse adherents may suggest that the guru was imparting divine energy to the recipient. Sometimes in the case of sexual abuse it is argued that the guru was trying to help the disciple overcome sexual drives by expressing them and not suppressing them. Anything can be ideologically worked out given the motive to keep one's worldview intact. Many religious stories actually illustrate ideological work at play.

Very often alterations occur without conscious intent simply with the retelling of the story in time. This is beautifully illustrated in the telephone game all of us remember playing as kids. You tell a story to someone, then they tell it to another and invariably something in the account has changed. The phrase "I like to eat pistachio nuts" somehow becomes "I go nuts for Picasso." Exaggeration is also an issue. On many occasions I have heard an outrageous surf story, usually about someone pearling down a twenty feet wave with tiger sharks nipping at their heels. But when confronting the initial source the admission comes that there were no scary monsters in the water and the wave was only four feet. How easy it is to add something extra so as to excite the next set of ears. With enough renditions the original account has been dramatically altered.

As for the symbolism, Carl Jung and Joseph Campbell contend that myths, much like dreams, reflect the archetypes (universal symbols) of the unconscious mind. A classic example of an archetype is the hero figure. In most (if not all) world religions there is a myth about a hero who faces some adversity, emerges transformed, and then serves as a symbol of strength and transcendence for others. Think of Moses, Nanak, Muhammad, Mahavira, the life of any religious figure. All of them encountered at some time or another a spiritual, political, or personal crisis and instead of succumbing to it they rose to the occasion. They become for us a symbol of hope, of what we too can be.

Sacred stories that are viewed as purely symbolic (at least from a modern and academic perspective) are the hundreds of creation accounts found throughout the world religions. Take, for instance, the Judeo-Christian creation myth. There are actually two separate creation stories in the Hebrew Scriptures: Genesis 1 and Genesis 2. According to biblical scholars both were oral stories passed down for nearly one thousand years before being officially recorded (many of the Jewish accounts were recorded in the 6th century B.C.E. when the Babylonians invaded and the Jews feared total annihilation of their culture).

Genesis 1 offers us the classic six-day creation account with god resting on the seventh day. Genesis 2, supposedly predating the former by hundreds of years and constructed by an entirely different school of thought, paints a more anthropomorphic god who interacts with the first humans, Adam and Eve. A fundamentalist Christian may ask what is symbolic here? Weren't these events historical? Well, to answer this it is important to understand the context in which these non-falsifiable accounts were developed. The authors were pre-scientific and so to grasp the origins of the universe they did not engage in any form of biological and cosmological research. As expected of tribal, preliterate, prerational people [9], they invoked rich symbolic imagery. For instance, the snake in Genesis 2 most likely was depicted as the symbol of evil since the Jewish people were often at odds with the Canaanites who used snakes in their form of worship. If we assume that the Jewish composers were giving an objective historical account of creation it becomes in a way an embarrassment for them. How easily the writers are proven wrong in light of modern scientific evidence. But if these particular Jewish myths are evaluated as containing a deeper meaning, as symbolic, they can be argued as valid and as true. Remember a symbol cannot be wrong. (Reformed Jews embrace this understanding.) Despite this awareness, to apply a critical analysis to one's own religious myths, especially if ingrained in one from childhood as history, takes a great deal of intellectual honesty and courage. To view another religion's myths as symbolic is usually not too difficult.

A Selection from the Hebrew Scriptures Explaining the Origin of Multiple Languages and Races in the Tower of Babel Story

"And the whole earth was of one language and of one speech... And they said one to another, Go to, let us make brick and burn them thoroughly. And they had brick for stone, and slime had they for mortar. And they said, Go to, let us build a city and a tower, whose top may reach unto heaven; and let us make us a name, lest we be scattered abroad upon the face of the whole earth. And the Lord came down to see the city and the tower, which the children of men built. And the Lord said, "Behold, the people is one, and they have all one language; and this they begin to do: and now nothing will be restrained from them which they have imagined to do. Go to, let us go down, and there confound their language, that they may not understand one another's speech. So the Lord scattered them abroad from thence upon the face of the earth..."

The Ritual Dimension: *Selection from Hsun Tzu's interpretation of Confucius on the Value of Rituals for Society* [10]

All too often religions critique other religions for being ritualistic. Protestants criticize Catholics for ceremonial grandeur; Muslims criticize the Christian community in general for its complicated forms of worship; Sikhs criticize Hindus for engaging in superfluous religious behavior, and the list continues. Some religions go as far as to say that they, unlike other traditions, do not engage in rituals at all. But in Religious Studies when we use the term ritual we mean it in a very benign way. Rituals are simply activities (usually repeated) that connect one with the sense of the sacred and all religions have them. Very often rituals are reenactments of religious myths. For Catholics administering the Eucharist is a reenactment of Jesus' last supper. However, rituals can be any action that imbues a feeling of transcendence. Meditating, praying, dancing as the Sufis do, chanting, singing religious hymns, reading religious literature, prostrating before sacred objects, attending religious services of any kind all fit under this category.

"Rites (referred to as li) rest on three bases: heaven and earth, which are the source of all life; the ancestor, who are the source of the human race; sovereigns and teachers, who are the source of government...It is through rites that Heaven and Earth are harmonious and sun and moon are bright, that the four seasons are ordered and the stars are on their courses, that river flow and that things prosper, that love and hatred are tempered and joy and anger are in keeping. They cause the lowly to be obedient and those on high to be illustrious. He who holds to rites is never confused in the midst of multifarious change; he who deviates there from is lost. Rites—are they not the culmination of culture?..."

The Experiential Dimension: *A Selection from the Bhagavad Gita, a sacred text for Hindus, where the poem's hero, Arjuna, experiences the glory of God* [11]

Hand in hand with rituals is the experiential dimension. It refers to the experience of the sacred, usually invoked via a ritual or spontaneously. For a brief moment, perhaps longer, engaging in a ritual can help one forgets one's self, one's troubles, and one's shortcomings, and connect with something greater. As stated earlier, whether these mystical encounters are insights into a higher reality accessible through our uncons- cious or superconscious mind or purely neurologically induced events, a byproduct of our brain chemistry, remains to be seen.

"I see You where ever I look—infinite your form! End, middle, or again beginning I cannot see in You, O Monarch Universal, manifest in every form!...How infinite your strength! How numberless your arms—yours eyes the sun and moon! So do I see You—your mouth a flaming fire, burning up this whole universe with your blazing glory. By You alone is this space between heaven and earth pervaded—all points of the compass too; gazing on this, your marvelous, frightening form, the three worlds shudder, All Highest Self!..."

The Doctrinal Dimension: *A Selection from the Samytta-Nikaya Explains Buddhism's Core Doctrine, the Eight Fold Path* [12]

The doctrines of a religion are the belief systems, the philosophies. These may be written down in a sacred text or orally transmitted. There is a thin line between the mythological dimension and the doctrinal one, for myths are intimately connected to the group's doctrines. Yet, doctrines are an attempt to offer a coherent system of beliefs beyond the symbolic language of myths. While the myth of the resurrection of Jesus is part of Christian doctrine, theologians do more than simply retell the story; they attempt to explain its significance.

"The Buddha said: What, monks, is the Nobel Eightfold Way? It is namely right view, right intention, right speech, right action, right livelihood, right effort, right mindfulness, right concentration. And what, monks, is right view? The knowledge of pain, knowledge of the cause of pain, knowledge of the cessation of pain, and knowledge of the way that leads to the cessation of pain...And what is right intention? The intentions to renounce, the intention not to hurt, the intention not to injure...And what is right speech? Refraining from falsehood, from malicious speech, from harsh speech, from frivolous speech...

And what is right action? Refraining from taking life; from taking what is not given, from sexual intercourse...And what is right livelihood? Here is a noble disciple abandoning a false mode of livelihood gets his living by right livelihood...And what is right effort? Here a monk with the non producing of bad and evil thoughts that have not yet arisen exercises will, puts efforts, begins to make exertion, applies and exerts his mind...And what is right mindfulness? Here on the body a monk abides contemplating the body, ardent, thoughtful, and mindful, dispelling his longing and dejection towards the world; on feelings he abides contemplating the feelings, ardent, thoughtful, and mindful, dispelling his longing and dejection towards the world; on thoughts he abides contemplating thoughts, ardent, thoughtful, and mindful, dispelling his longing and dejection toward the world. And what is right concentration? Here a monk is free from passions and evil thoughts attains and abides in the first trance of joy and pleasure, which is accompanied by reasoning and investigation and arises from seclusion. With the ceasing of reasoning and investigation, in a state of internal serenity, with his mind fixed on one point, he attains and abides in the second trance of joy and pleasure arising from concentration...With equanimity and indifference towards joy he abides mindful and self-possessed, and with his body experiences pleasure that the noble ones call "dwelling with equanimity, mindful and happy" and attains and abides in the third trance. Dispelling pleasure and pain, and even before the disappearance of elation and depression, he attains and abides in the fourth trance, which is without pleasure and pain and with the purity of mindfulness and equanimity..."

The Ethical Dimension: *A Selection from the Akaranga-sutra Illustrates Jain Ahimsa (Non-Violence) and Respect for Life* [13]

Religions contain a code of ethics. The ethical behavior of the dominant religion usually controls society. For instance, in America, where Judeo-Christian values are predominant, there is little attention paid to the morality of eating animals, whereas in India, with a vast Hindu population, vegetarianism is common. There are a few ethical standards that seem to be universal, however. Most societies (if not all) do not allow murder, lying, cheating, stealing, and promote some form of the Golden Rule: treat others as you wish to be treated. This moral pronouncement is found in the teachings of Jesus, Buddha, Confucius, and others. The psychologist Lawrence Kohlberg argues that there are developmental stages of morality: pre-moral (infants with no sense of morality yet), egoistic (totally self-centered), social approval (concerned with recognition), law and order (following rules rigorously), fair and justice (focus on what is inherently right), and the Golden Rule stage. Though many religions may have their ideal set at the highest level of morality, in actuality Kohlberg contends few of us live up to this standard.

"All beings with two, three, four, or five sense,...in fact all creation know individually pleasure and displeasure, pain, terror and sorrow. All are full of fears which come from all directions. And yet there exist people who would cause greater pain to them...Some kill animals for sacrifice, some for their skin, flesh, blood,...feathers, teeth, tusks;...some kill them intentionally...He who harms animals has not understood or renounced deeds of sin...He who understands the nature of sin against animals is called a rue sage who understands karma..A man who is adverse from harming even the wind knows the sorrow of all things living...He who knows what is bad for himself knows what is bad for others, and he who knows what is bad for others knows what is bad for himself. This reciprocity should always be borne in mind. Those whose minds are at peace and who are free from passions do not desire to live at the expense of others..."

The Social Dimension: Estimated Numbers in the Major World Religions

Religions have a communal aspect and some form of organization. My independent, idiosyncratic philosophy does not constitute a religion since it lacks this social ele- ment. While there is no magical threshold number to constitute a religion, certainly a religion is more than one person's philosophical meandering. The organization surrounding a religion can be extremely complex as with the Catholic Church or very loose knit as we see with religions originating on the internet. In the case of the latter, religious ideas are espoused on the computer screen and a following (however small) can emerge. Instead of attending churches, members visit web sites and chat rooms.

Overall, the social dimension of religion allows for a sense of normative values and group bonding. Sociologists of religion, such as Emile Durkheim, Bryan Wilson, and Georg Simmel, argue from a functionalist standpoint that religions are a necessary component of a well functioning society since they supply it with not only rules to live by but, most importantly, a community to live in.

Buddhism: Approximately three hundred million Buddhists worldwide

Sikhism: Approximately twenty million Sikhs worldwide

Hinduism: Approximately eight hundred million Hindus worldwide

Jainism: Approximately three to four million Jains worldwide

Islam: Approximately eight to nine hundred million Muslims worldwide

Judaism: Approximately fifteen to sixteen million Jews worldwide

Christianity: Approximately two billion Christians worldwide, with half of that being Catholic

The Material Dimension: Examples of Religious Material Forms

The final element of religion is the material dimension. This includes any materials that help connect the believer to the sacred. Books, buildings, clothing, and other physical forms with religious meaning fit here. In religious studies a material object that is viewed as a direct manifestation or embodiment of the sacred is termed a hierophany. For Christians it can be a Bible; for Sikhs it can be the Adi Granth; for Hindus it can be the guru himself/herself. A hierophany not only serves as a conduit to the divine, it itself is viewed as transcendent.

Buddhism: Stupas, graceful towers that house sacred relics and sometimes ashes of a Buddhist saint

Sikhism: The Golden Temple located in Amritsar, the central religious site for Sikhs

Hinduism: Shiva Lingum shaped in the form of a phallus, a religious artifact that represents fertility and creation

Jainism: The Monk himself viewed as a symbol of enlightenment

Islam: The Kaaba located in Mecca, a place all Muslims are expected to pilgrimage to sometime in their lives

Judaism: The Torah, otherwise known as the Pentateuch, which contains the first five books of the Hebrew Scriptures

Christianity: The Cross symbolizing the death of Jesus for the redemption of souls

NOTES

1.   See Mircea Eliade's *Sacred and Profane: The Nature of Religion* (Chicago: University of Chicago Press, 1959).

2.   See Rudolph Otto's *Idea of the Holy*, 2nd ed., tr. By John W. Harvey (New York: 1950).

3.   By agnosticism let me clarify that I do not mean that I entertain all ontological systems as possibilities. In fact, I can honestly say that I do not embrace any. Acknowledging the limitations of the human mind in grasping Reality, whatever that may be, more accurately defines my position.

4.   Richard Dawkins, *Unweaving the Rainbow: Science, Delusion and the Appetite for Wonder* (New York: Houghton Mifflin Co., 1998), p. x.

5.   From *The World As I See It*, 1934.

6.   I was fortunate enough to have Ninian Smart serve as my M.A. and Ph.D. chairperson on my graduate committee at UC Santa Barbara. His friendly smile and jovial character was very appreciated during those highly stressed times preparing papers and studying for exams.

7.   See Ninan Smart's *The Religious Experience* (New York: Macmillan Publishing Co., 1991).

8.   For a case example see *Da: The Strange Case of Franklin Jones* by Scott Lowe and David Lane (Walnut: MSAC Philosophy Group, 1995).

9.   According to Ken Wilber, a noted transpersonal psychologist, tribal people fit in the prerational category as they lack a cause and effect worldview, relying mainly on magic and symbolism.

10.   Passage is found in Lewis Hopfe's *Religions of the World* (New York: Macmillan Publishing Co., 1991), pp. 241-42.

11.   Passage is found in *Religions of the World*, p. 133.

12.   Passage is found in *Religions of the World*, pp. 179-81.

13.   Passage is found in *Religions of the World*, p. 150.

Where Did Religion Come From?

The Biological Explanation

My first direct or personal encounter with a materialist, scientific explanation for the origin of religion occurred in 1987 when I was finishing up my undergraduate work at the University of California, San Diego. I was invited to attend a faculty party at the house of the well-known neuroscientist and psychologist, Professor Ramachandran (a.k.a. Rama). Since the gathering commenced at 8 p.m., I decided to arrive fashionably late, around 9 p.m., so as to blend into the crowd and not be too noticeable. I guess I was intimidated being the only undergraduate asked to go. Well, everyone seemed to have had the same plan, except they were going for the 9:15 or 9:30 slot. So lo and behold I was actually the first guest to arrive, perhaps an omen that an embarrassing evening was on its way. The next person to show up was a tall, elder gentleman introduced to me by Rama as Francis. His wife, I was told, was a famous painter and her artwork was celebrated on Rama's walls. Francis and I sat on the couch chit chatting while more and more guests came. I could not help but notice all eyes were in our direction. I wondered whether my new hairstyle was drawing attention. Maybe my new outfit was exceptionally groovy. Cameras occasionally flashed and enthusiastic guests hovered nearby. Still all the while I was clueless who this Francis was? I conversed with him for over two hours on a variety of topics, from animal rights to religion. Had I known this was one the most famous scientists in the twentieth century, that he had received the Nobel Prize in chemistry, that books were written about him and an HBO movie was made on him, I don't think I would have dared to speak so freely and so relaxed. It was none other than Francis Crick, the Cambridge scientist who discovered the structure of the DNA molecule and who is considered one the original architects of genetics. I did not discover his identity until the next day when Rama called me to say he took a photo of Francis Crick and me together. When I learned of whom my social partner was, my mind frantically reviewed the discussion. What did I say? Cold sweat began to bead on my forehead and my hands started to tremble. Did I really ask Francis Crick what he did for a living? When he vaguely retorted that he "dabbled in a little bit of this and that" I suspected he meant janitorial work. Had I actually suggested that if he had nothing going on he could come down to Rama's lab and help me with the research on visual perception? Was I too nervy when I argued with him over the morality of vegetarianism and poked his shoulder in protest to his argument as he did mine? I could not turn a darker shade of red if I tried. While it makes a great story, how I wish I could go back and respectfully appreciate one of the great minds of the twentieth century. Yet, I doubt if I had known who he was I would have had enough audacity to talk so openly. The sly grin on his face gave me the impression he was enjoying his disguise. Perhaps that is why he stayed seated on the couch next to (in this context) the dumb blond for the duration of the party instead of mingling with the gloating onlookers.

I learned a lot about Crick that night, including his views on religion and God. From his perspective as a neuroscientist, everything, from our thoughts to our actions to our beliefs, can be explained by what is going on inside the brain. Even the notion of free will is neurologically based. As for religion, Crick contended it too is a bio-product of our brain chemistry [1]. It does not come from God, from some higher, mystical reality, but from the construction of our neural network. Religion has emerged since our neurology allows us to contemplate the mysteries of the universe by asking why and how type questions. Without a certain amount of neurons and neuronal connections there would never be religion to begin with. The reason why we do not speak of dog religions or bird religions is because they do not possess the necessary neurological state for it.

Why did we neurologically develop the notion of religion in the first place? The materialist interpretation for the origin of religion really begins with an understanding of evolutionary biology. According to evolutionists, the goal of nature is to pass on one's genes. When the code of one's DNA mixes with another's, there are random changes or mutations that can occur, some minor and some more significant. If this change is to the benefit of the organism (that is, it allows it to live a longer life and hence reproduce more) then it is passed on. The environment does not determine the change itself but plays a decisive role in determining which changes will be considered beneficial. For instance, if a baby finch is born with a more pointed and longer beak than its competitors and happens to habitat a very wet area this animal has a greater chance of survival than the others as it could dig deeper into the soggy soil for food. Since it is eating better than most this bird is expected to live a longer life. It will then have more opportunities for reproduction and its genes will potentially dominate the next generation. Yet, if the same animal were born in a dry area we would most likely see only a few of its descendants, if any, for a pointed, long beak is a disadvantage in this condition.

A fairly new discipline in evolutionary studies is evolutionary psychology. Scholars here claim that the very thoughts we think can play a role in our survival. As an example, possessing the idea of love (brotherly love, motherly love, or romantic love) is to our evolutionary advantage. Offering love and support to a sibling or friend allows for camaraderie, hence a decline of individual existential angst and an incentive to live a full life. Since the mother feels love for her young she will nurture them and maintain their existence. When a male feels love (and/or lust) for a women reproduction can occur. Overall, it is apparent that the idea of love is helpful for our continuation.

Now let us apply this to religion. According to evolutionary psychologists, religion itself is an important survival tool for our species. It offers many powerful benefits, including a sense of meaning, group cohesion, and social rules. Instead of existential dread one's life seems to have a point; instead of social disarray one's community has order. Thus, early humans who possessed a religious outlook of some kind may have had a greater chance of survival. While the surface structures of religion may vary from one group to another (there are a variety of religious orientations in the world) the overall deep structure of religion remains embedded within our consciousness today. Serving as a survival mechanism for our ancestors, religion is not so easily forgotten.

The Theological Explanation

Besides the biological explanation, there are other theories about how and why religion began offered by theologians, anthropologists, psychologists, and sociologists. Let us start with the theological position since it is generally the simplest to understand. From this perspective, religion originated from the

Divine. God (however one fashions It) imparted spiritual truths to various mystics, prophets, or seers at some time or another and these revelations were then preserved (usually orally in the beginning) in a sacred book. In addition to the religious literature, believers can partake in the transcendent through religious rituals, generally orchestrated or monitored by a clergy member.

For Jews religion came from Yahweh; for Muslims religion came from Allah; for Christians religion came from the Trinity (note: essentially Yahweh, Allah and the Father of the Trinity refer to the same deity); for Hindus religion came from one of the millions of gods or goddesses or from the impersonal, mystical reality, Brahman; for Jains and Buddhists religion came from a higher understanding (note: Mahayana Buddhists do accept a celestial notion of the Buddha); etc. According to the theological position the bottom line is: religion has a transcendent origin.

As a child I was indoctrinated in the Christian perspective. Sister Enda, Sister Mary Francis, Sister Lucy and all of the other nuns at Our Lady of Lourdes School started and ended each class session with a prayer recognizing God's hand in the day and thanking this Being for guidance. That God existed and interacted with humans was presupposed; that religion, specifically theirs, was a valid means to relate to God was also assumed. Very specific rules were reinforced to ensure proper etiquette with this God. When I happened to forget my beanie on a day the class was attending church, the sisters would bobby pin a piece of tissue or toilet paper square on my head so that God would not be offended (remember this was the mid-seventies when women were generally expect to wear veils to mass). I think it was also a way to embarrass me so that in the future I would not be so negligent. The fact that I repeatedly had Kleenex or Charmin on my head indicates that plan did not seem to work.

Obviously there is really no way for the academic to verify the theological position--that one's religion came from God--mainly because the claim of God's existence is itself non-testable and is beyond the realm of science. Hence, all the social scientists can do with it is to acknowledge it as a matter of faith.

The Anthropological Explanation

Coming from this Catholic heritage I remember the many miracle stories that circulated about holy objects. The Eucharist when treated improperly was said to bleed; water when blessed was said to cure ailments; wooden crosses were said to ward off evil spirits; special statues were said to shed tears; and on occasion in tortillas the Virgin Mary was said to appear. While with Occam's razor we can offer simpler, alternative, naturalistic explanations of these phenomena, the animistic concepts here are apparent. In all religions we find some aspect of animism-- material forms taking on a life of their own as they imbued a spiritual power.

E.B. Tylor, a 19th century British anthropologist, advanced the theory that religion originated from animism [2]. Primal people, according to Tylor, developed the belief that spirit forces exist and can embody particular objects such as a rock or a tree. The notion of spirits occurred when they mistook the apparitions of a dream, usually of dead ancestors, as visions of spirit entities. Spirits were then projected unto animals and material objects in nature and rituals were invoked to interact with and control them. Simply put, from dreams came the idea of spirits, from spirits came the idea of animism, and religion with its myths and rituals followed.

Another popular anthropological explanation for the origin of religion comes from Sir James Frazer, a 19th – early 20th century British scholar. He argued that for early human beings religion initially grew out of magic [3]. With the lack of a scientific worldview, the forces of nature were reckoned with through magical formulations. Eventually, since magic did not help primal people control the environment effectively, these impersonal forces became deified as personal gods (it was easier to manipulate something with a name and a personality than unpredictable, indifferent powers that be) and religion then began. Thus, religion is a step in the evolution of human intellect. The next step, claimed Frazer, is science. A religious explanation of the world will no longer suffice as science offers a much more powerful tool for understanding and controlling nature [4].

The Psychological Explanation

Since I majored in psychology I ran into Sigmund Freud's and Carl Jung's name quite a bit. Whenever Freud's theories were discussed in class up came the topic of sex. Often the class atmosphere turned uncomfortable as the Oedipus and Electra complex were entertained. Repulsed by the idea of one's mother or father as a sexual partner most students grinned their teeth and let out a "ugh" sound. Well, as expected Freud also connects the origin of religion to sex. According to Freud, religion stems from deep psychological roots of our unconscious mind [5]. Early male humans, out of passion for their mother and jealousy of their father (otherwise known as the Oedipus complex), wished the father dead. Instead of carrying out the act in reality they substituted an animal and performed a sacrifice in a ritual ceremony. The animal became the totem for the particular clan and taboos were established concerning it. Totemism, then, is the first form of religion announced Freud [6].

His student, Jung, whose overall psychological analysis deviated a great deal from his mentor, agreed with Freud that religion comes from our unconscious mind but disagreed that it has a neurotic genesis. Rather, Jung declared that our "collective" unconscious mind is filled with archetypal symbols, many of which manifest in our dream state, and religion is an outward expression of them. Tapping into the deeper meaning of religious symbolism can lead one to a higher understanding of the universe. Joseph Campbell, a scholar of mythology, certainly agreed with this thesis as he dedicated his life to comparing religious myths and unraveling the psychological significance buried within them.

The Sociological Explanation

Sociologists of religion approach this subject from a very different angle. According to this school of thought, religion does not have purely a psychological origin but a social one. Emile Durkheim, a 19th century scholar considered one of the original thinkers of sociology, agreed with Freud that the first form of religion for early tribal humans was totemism. But unlike Freud who saw the totem as a substitute for the father, for Durkheim the totem was a personification of the forces of society [7]. Surrounded the totem were certain rules of society (taboos) that were empowered as they were associated with something that seemed to transcend the mundane realm. Religions of today follow the same dynamic. Instead of a totem animal we speak of God. Yet, this entity is none other than the embodiment of societal elements at play. God sets up how we are to behave and what we are to think. This allows for social order. When disobeying the rules one is threatened with an existence in hell (or, if from an eastern perspective, a bad rebirth), demanding no less than total obedience.

There is an interesting story I read about in the Los Angeles Times illustrating the extent of religion's grip over what we think and how we act. It is about a Hindu man who sued Taco Bell for mixing up his food order. Instead of the vegetarian bean burrito he requested the clerk handed him a beef one. A couple of bites later he informed his wife that the burrito had a flavor he had never tasted before. When he unraveled the flour tortilla to his horror he discovered meat. Now, while a vegetarian diet has no necessary connection to religious ideology (there are many non-religious vegetarians) in this context it did. His lawsuit was based on the claim that he was now considered impure to other Hindus and that bad karma was heading his way. A painful illness? A detrimental rebirth? Only fate could tell. Eventually, the lawsuit was settled out of court. The point of the story has nothing to do with what to order or not to order at Taco Bell. Rather it suggests that for this devotee disobeying the religious rules he was raised with meant for him severe social and spiritual consequences (and perhaps in this case a cushy financial benefit).

Besides offering normative values and an incentive to honor them, religion creates a feeling of belonging for its constituents. During religious services adherents usually greet each other, hold hands during prayers, sing together, and afterwards plan social events. Two years ago a woman in my class confessed to me that she no longer believed in her religious upbringing but grieved over the loss of the social community. So torn up was she that for about a year she still attended the services just to feel a part of a group until the ideological differences became too irreconcilable. From then on her social calendar was no longer the same.

The anthropologist Victor Turner argued that religion offers a unique sense of *communitas*, an academic term simply meaning community. During religious rituals, such as pilgrimages, social distinctions are ignored, hierarchies leveled, and *communitas* experienced. A classic example occurs during the Muslim's pilgrimage to Mecca. All pilgrims strip themselves of ornaments, including jewelry, fantasy clothes, and makeup, and wear plain white cotton attire with sandals. There are no doctors, lawyers, shop owners, mechanics, clerks, beggars, but attending are one class of people—followers of Allah. Returning to society the disciple feels reinvigorated, as though one can face the everyday grind and accept one's social disposition, whatever that be, with a smile. Social order and cohesion, necessary requirements for a healthy society, are reestablished.

Explanations for Religion

Biological: Religion developed as a survival mechanism.

Theological: Religion comes from God.

Anthropological: Religion can be understood when examining the thought process of primal humans; it began with animism or a deification of the forces of nature.

Psychological: Religion originates from our unconscious mind.

Sociological: Religion has social origins.

Egotistical: Religion, in some special cases, is a conscious formulation so as to garner for its creator praise and income.

A More Cynical Explanation

Thus far we have been reviewing why the religious mind developed. Another question to ask is why would one found a religion to begin with. Of course, there are many authentically inspired religious teachers; one only has to consider Buddha, Jesus, Muhammad, although it could be argued that their disciples, not themselves, founded the tradition that followed. However, there are some religions that seem to have a more dubious origin. Instead of driven by a feeling of divine calling, the incentive to start the group may be for alternative reasons, including fame and fortune.

Understanding the seven dimensions that constitutes a religion allows us to see how easy it is to create one. If one covers all the bases and includes myths, rituals, a code of ethics, etc., one can develop one's own movement. While I am in no way arguing that all religions are a conscious creation of opportunists (there are many sincere and uplifting traditions), certainly several may be. There are hundreds, if not thousands, of cases of religions, especially new religions, which fit under this category [8]. Manufacturing a religion takes some creativity, usually a great deal of ego and a lot of time on one's hands. (I figure if I burn out of teaching another more profitable career awaits me.) It also takes an audience. P.T. Barnum's statement that "a sucker is born every minute" addresses many of the constituents here. The making of a spiritual movement is made simpler today more than ever due to the Internet--an accessible tool to get the message out. In time, if enough people find the ideas appealing, there will be an incentive to write more books, to develop fascinating hagiography, to record numinous experiences, to fine tune doctrines, to clarity moral systems, and the fledgling movement can really begin to take off.

Yet, whatever the religion's origins, whether genuinely or materialistically inspired, the fact remains that from the perspective of the disciple a sense of the sacred, perhaps an inherent trait of humans, is somehow touched. Even for the most charlatan of religions what the members bring to it from their own desires, hopes, and experiences can give the group a transformative quality.

A Combination Approach

As we have seen, there are many interesting explanations for the origin of religion. Determining which one is more valid is difficult. Perhaps religion's beginnings can be understood only when combining the different approaches. For instance, the archetypes Jung and Campbell speak of, which may have survival benefits, may fit nicely into the evolutionary psychology camp. And the step out of the magical world into the religious one that Frazer mentions may have resulted from an advancement in neurology (new neural connections means a new world view). Or if one wishes one could declare from a perspective of faith that religion initially came from tapping into the realm of the transcendent and perhaps dreams offered the window to do this. The special cases of religion being willfully created for opportunist reasons should also be considered. However one explains religion's origins, there is one thing we can feel confident in: religion will most likely have a prosperous future since it is so deeply rooted in our neurology and hence psychology. The claim that secularization will eventually overtake religion remains suspect at this stage. We will investigate the future of religion in the final section of this book.

NOTES

1.   See Francis Crick's *The Astonishing Hypothesis: The Scientific Search for the Soul*.

2.   See E.B. Tylor's *Primitive Culture* (published in 1871).

3.   The anthropological viewpoint suggests that to understand the origin of religion one should study the evolution of the human intellect. The mindset of primal human beings is key because it marks the first stage of it. Since we cannot go back thousands of years ago to investigate early humans many anthropologists examine present day tribal people who are untouched by civilization.

4.   See Sir James Frazer's *The New Golden Bough: A New Abridgment of Sir James Frazer's Classic Work*, by Theodor H. Gaster (New York: 1959).

5.   Freud also made the argument that God (at least in the Western religions) was nothing but a projection of our own earthly father onto a superhuman figure. See Freud's *Future of an Illusion* (New York: 1976).

6.   For Freud's view on the origin of religion see his *Totem and Taboo* published in 1912-1913 (the English translation appeared in 1918).

7.   See Emile Durkheim's *The Elementary Forms of the Religious Life*. Translated from the French by J.W. Swain (London: Allen and Unwin, 1976).

8.   Paul Twitchell's Eckankar is a case in point. For more information see David Lane's *The Making of a Spiritual Movement: The Untold Story of Paul Twitchell* (Del Mar: Del Mar Press, 1983).

Why Study Religion?

When I ask my students why they signed up for a religion course I get the typical answer: "Because it's a G.E." Sometimes students confess their strong religious background and their desire to learn about other religions so as to strengthen their belief in their own. It is rare that I hear one say simply because this is a darn interesting topic. When I am graced with such a response I can't help but feel a bit stoked. As might be expected, from my perspective religion is one of the most fascinating of subjects. It has been around since the beginning of the primal world and it still permeates our society in all its multifarious forms. Religion informs our thoughts, structures our world, and determines our culture. To ignore this subject is to dismiss a significant aspect of the human being and of the world at large.

Studying world religions can also help build a more tolerant individual and society. The more we learn about something foreign usually the greater the affinity we have for it. I remember taking a course in African literature in my sophomore year at UCSD and developing a craving to visit Africa. It no longer was a scary continent filled with Ebola viruses but a rich tapestry of different counties with beautiful poetry and charming folklore. When something is totally new to us there is a tendency to label it "strange" or "weird." Learning about how Vedanta Hindus meditate, why Tibetan Buddhists spin the prayer wheel, or the significance of Muslims going on a pilgrimage to Mecca can develop an appreciation for them. The student of religion can burst through the tunnel vision they have been imprisoned in and see the world from entirely new perspectives. Hopefully, empathy can replace provincialism. Perhaps at the semester's end one's worldview remains undaunted but at least one had the opportunity to stretch one's mind in fresh directions.

On a few occasions students identify with one particular philosophy and pursued an affiliation with the respective group. A couple of semesters ago on my evaluation day with the Dean observing the class four students entered with Hare Krishna haircuts (shaved with a tuft in the back). These male students were not interested in becoming Hare Krishas per se but after interviewing members of the group and learning that the hairstyle symbolized renunciation of the material world they decided to make a similar statement, perhaps in rebellion against yuppie culture. When pushed further they admitted that they thought the hair cut was "cool." But when one of my students recently dropped out of school, gave away all his possessions, and flew to Alaska to meditate and to search for Truth, inspired by the life of the Indian mystic Ramana Maharshi, I think he may have taken the material a little too seriously. I cannot help but feel a little guilty since he read Ramana's autobiography in my class. Overall, however, the assignment to visit other religious centers allows students an opportunity to interact with the subject they are reading about in books. Very often friendships are formed and students on their own return to the site for worship, discussion, or a friendly meal.

Thus, the study of world religions can tear down unnecessary social divisions. How one interacts with others may be affected now that one understands why Indian women wear a bright dot on their forehead, why Jains refuse to eat meat, or why traditional male Sikhs carry a dagger. Having learned the greetings of the many religions several students report a great thrill in addressing devotees with them, whether at the work place or local bus stop. For instance, the Indian greeting is "Namaste," translated as "I bow to the Divine in you." (Hindus revere all life forms as a part of the Divine.) Last year a female student revealed how pleased she was to greet an Indian customer in her checkout line with the phrase. For a brief moment in her life she bonded with someone of a totally different background and orientation.

Furthermore, many misconceptions can be shattered in this course. One realizes that very few Muslims are terrorists, that Wicca has no connection to Satanism, that Hindus do not worship the cow, and that there is not one Christian religion but almost one thousand different Christian groups. By appearance students commonly mistake Islamic Saudi women for Hindu women and turban-wearing male Sikhs for Hindu males. Recognizing the classic symbolic attire for each group (yamakas for male Jews, silver bracelets for male Sikhs, saris for Hindu women, nudity for certain male Jain monks, etc.) lessens the chance to misidentify and to offend.

Never before has the study of religion been so necessary. Living in the pluralistic world that we do, sometimes referred to as a "global village," we have the opportunity to interact with faiths and cultures from around the world in our own hometown. One has only to walk down the boardwalk in Laguna Beach on a Sunday afternoon to observe a Christian preacher offering quotes from the New Testament, Hare Krishnas in orange or white attire joyfully chanting with tambourines in hand near the basket ball courts, and Buddhist monks wearing brown robes and with clean shaven heads gingerly walking with great mindfulness. Today's global village is the result of technology. Travel to foreign countries and communication with them is now available at record speed. No longer are we distinct clans separated by geography but we resemble a colorful collage of faces that if looked at closer blend into one.

America's pluralism flourished in the 1960s when L.B. Johnson rescinded the immigration restriction laws set back in the 1920s. The reason they were established in the first place was because immigrants were given I.Q. tests when they entered this country and most failed. That the tests were in English and usually administered in crowded conditions explains why the scores were below par. Nonetheless, it was argued that "moron" blood was entering into America and the interbreeding with Americans was bringing down American intelligence. When Calvin Coolidge bought the argument few immigrants were allowed access to US soil. This certainly hurt German Jews seeking refuge during WWII. For decades America was essentially a Judeo-Christian nation of Caucasian predominance. Then in 60s the landscape changed as numerous foreigners were allowed to make America their home. We witness the onslaught of Indian teachers and an increased interest in mediation and eastern philosophy at this time. Moreover, centers of the world's religions were springing up throughout this country. Of course, America already had some Buddhist and Hindu temples, Islamic mosques, and other distinct places of worship but these were few and far between. Today, thirty-five years later, the society we live in is vibrant with all different types of religious organizations, from Bahai to Scientology to Sufism to Gnosticism to traditional forms of religion.

Finally, and perhaps most importantly, one should study religion and philosophy in general simply to be a well-informed, educated person. That is the whole point of G.E. classes—they are considered so important for a well-rounded education that they are required. To graduate college thinking that Muslim and Islam refer to distinct religions (Muslim refers to one who follows Islam) or that Hindus are all polytheists (many are pure monists) would be an indication that the educational program was not complete. Think how embarrassing of a social faux pas it could be while in the work place a lawyer gives one's Islamic partner a ham sandwich during a luncheon or when brokering a business deal one serves meatloaf to a Jain businessman. One is not simply studying religion but cultural values and how to properly address others.

Overall, the study of religion is a benefit to both the individual and to society. This discipline creates a better informed and hopefully more tolerant person. Each step taken in this direction adds to a world that is a bit more livable and less prone to bigotry and intolerance. While wars may not cease at least the religious affiliated ones may be somewhat diminished. While parents will still be hyper critical about whom their daughter is dating perhaps they won't freak out when they find out he is of a different faith. While in the job market where there is a rigorous screening process maybe the hiring committee will find the Hindu women in sari attire a fascinating asset to the company. Religion is so much a part of our lives affecting our politics, our relations, our place in society, it needs to be taken seriously.

How Should We Study Religion?

Having pursued an M.A. and Ph.D. in Religious Studies I have been asked on many occasions why I did. Several have queried if I was planning on entering the religious life (Sister Andrea Grace? I don't think so). Others have questioned what I could do with such a degree, and why I would even bother to study this subject. In a world where most students pursue very practical degrees such as business, nursing, or accounting, these are valid questions. But there is a great deal of misconception about what Religious Studies entails. Scholars in this field are not interested in studying religion as believers of it, pondering what is the Truth, for this falls outside of an objective study. Rather, they investigate religion as historians, sociologists, and cultural anthropologists. For instance, Buddhist scholars would not be concerned with how to attain Nirvana for their personal liberation, but with what Nirvana means to Buddhists. They would also have an interest in the different types of Buddhist schools, what each group believes in, how certain Buddhist ideas originated, and the effects of Buddhist ideas on culture and society at large.

Often confused with Religious Studies is Theology, yet there is a fundamental difference between the two. Theology approaches religion from an insider's view--that is, as a believer. Many theologians actually enter religious vocation. The existence of God, the truth of religion, and the validity of alternative religions are all topics here. While several past and present theologians have offered a great deal to our understanding of religion (certainly theologian Paul Tillich's contribution should not be ignored), it is not Religious Studies. Unlike theologians who address religion with a religious viewpoint, scholars of religion may be agnostics, total atheists, or themselves religious. In this area one's religious orientation is of no consequence because as historians the objective is to analyze the origins and content of philosophical groups without addressing the truth-value of them. Thus, the professional goal of a Religious Studies scholar is not to be a member of the clergy or of a theological board but generally to be a researcher, writer, and professor of the subject.

I learned the difference between Theology and Religious Studies the hard way. After obtaining my B.A. in Psychology from UCSD I entered graduate school at USD in Theology. I was interested in the effects of religion on society and did not realize that I entered the wrong area to study this. Figuring this out shortly into the semester I submitted an application to UCSB's Religious Studies program and was admitted for the following year. Unfortunately, this was only after I paid a very high tuition at USD for ten units that did not transfer.

The Study of Religion

Theology: The study of religion from a believer's perspective; theological questions concern the idea of religious truth

Religious Studies: This refers to the academic study of religion from a more secular viewpoint; scholars in this field need not be religious; the overall goal is the objective study of religion; the following disciplines in this box find a place in Religious Studies

Phenomenology: A purely descriptive approach to religious phenomena; a phenomenologist attempts to step into the shoes of the believer when collecting data on the religion so as to do justice to the subject

Sociology of Religion: The scholar here wants to understand the social origins of religion; besides collecting data about the religion the sociologists attempts to analyze how ideas developed in a human, historical context; reduction is associated with this discipline

Psychology of Religion: The study of the religious mind--what makes one religious and what are the psychological effects of religion

History of Religion: The historian of religion is interested in the historical happenings associated with the religion: dates, places, events are all discussed; as an historian one may utilize the sociological explanations to comprehend the social origins of the topic

34

Anthropology of Religion: Anthropology is the study of humans, and this includes religion; in evaluating the culture of a group religion is often key; cultural anthropologists often study primal religions so as to understand how and why early humans developed religion in the first place; ethnographic studies is usually the method use

While at UCSB I studied under Ninian Smart, one of the world's foremost scholars of religion. In a seminar on methodology Smart suggested that there are three main ways to study religion: with antipathy, with sympathy, and with empathy. The first method, embraced by Freud and perhaps Marx, looks at religion with scorn as primitive and childish, as a sort of pariah on society. Freud called religion a neurosis and suggested we need to be healed from it. Marx was critical of capitalism, and religion, he asserted, perpetuated it. Oppressed creatures turn to religion for comfort and hence fail to revolt; religion then is a tool to prevent social change and to maintain the status quo. The second method is embraced by theologians. Here one presupposes the truth of religion and generally evaluates other religions as lesser versions of the right one. As expected, Smart and other academicians in Religious Studies support the latter approach since it seems to be much less biased. Instead of religion being cursed or hailed the goal here is to try to step into the shoes of the subject at hand and see the world from that viewpoint. For instance, when reporting on a tribe in Africa the scholar observes and may even partake in the rituals as a social scientist collecting data and then descriptively documents the event as objectively as possible. The empathetic approach has a scholarly title; it is referred to as *phenomenology--* the objective, descriptive study of religious phenomena.

In the seminar the question surfaced whether a truly objective study could be possible since all of us have some form of bias to begin with? Karl Mannheim, a sociologist of religion, argues that the scholar, even if one wanted to, can never really be totally objective, since one is a product of a particular historical existence and so evaluates data based on frames of reference or categories of a given historical moment [1]. Smart responded to the query by saying, "Well, while all of us may be sinners there are certainly degrees of sin." In other words, there is a big difference between a totally prejudice study and one that tries to keep as much bias as possible in check. To collapse the distinction is a category error.

Maintaining objectivity and empathy is sometimes not an easy task. When I first traveled to India I recall being shocked when I saw a poor Indian girl begging for change with only half a hand. I learned that her fingers had probably been cut off when she was a baby by her parents. Though a rarity, there are cases of this happening among the lowest caste in India. Of course, from a Western standpoint it was barbaric. Yet, let us step into the shoes of the participants. If you had a child whose social position was destined to be a beggar (remember there is no social climbing in the caste system), you would probably want to ensure that he or she is the best beggar on the block. It is a simple matter of survival. Deformations usually bring sympathy and hence more donations from tourists. In a strange way the parents were looking out for the girl. The lesson here is that we need to understand the social environment in total before passing final judgment.

Smart's Three Approaches to Study Religion

Antipathy: A negative view of religion; an attempt to unmask the distortion of religion

Sympathy: Generally a positive, yet biased view of religion; an assumption of the truth of religion; often a critical view of "other" religions outside of one's own

Empathy: A neutral view of religion; an attempt to understand religion from the subject's perspective so as to properly describe it; this method wins the support of Smart

Peter Berger, a well-known scholar of religion, agrees with Smart that there are three approaches to religion. Instead of antipathy, sympathy and empathy he refers to them as reduction, deduction and induction [2]. Reduction has a slightly different meaning than antipathy, however. Religion is not dismissed as a leviathan of society but viewed as a product of material culture and reduced down to its material underpinnings. The goal then is to unmask the social origins of religion. Identical with the sympathetic approach, deduction is an attempt to reassert religious certainty, to deduce religious truths (Theology fits here). And in parallel with empathy, the inductive approach, phenomenological at heart, concentrates on the experiential side of religion.

Berger's Three Approaches to Study Religion

Reduction: An attempt to reduce religion to its social origins; a classic method of sociologists of religion

Deduction: Similar to Smart's sympathetic approach and to theology; an assumption of religious truth as in neo-orthodoxy

Induction: A phenomenological approach to religion; an attempt to take seriously the religious experience of the believer and to describe it accordingly without presupposing its ontological truth; this method wins the support of Berger

According to Berger, the phenomenological approach is the best option because it allows an air of openness between scholar and devotee and greater insight into the religion in question. However, I would argue that his rebuff of reduction for not taking seriously the religious claim is altogether premature, for it is a very powerful and necessary method to study religion and should work in conjunction with induction. While phenomenology is indeed an important process to study religion, it is only half of it. Along with gathering the data one must critically analyze it. The word critical here should not be confused with criticism; critical in this context means to evaluate the data with a scientific mindset [3]. Again, objectivity is crucial. Simply describing religious phenomena and not analyzing its origins, its deeper meaning, its effect on the society in question would not suffice. Otherwise known as the sociology of religion, the reductive approach is valuable precisely because it is able to ground religion in a social context and evaluate it accordingly.

To put this all in perspective, induction/phenomenology works in this field only in combination with reduction/sociology of religion: the former is important when data collecting, while the later is required for critical analysis. Phenomenology supplies us with the *whats* -- what are the beliefs, what are the rituals and myths, etc -- whereas sociology of religion gives us the hows and whys -- how and why did these develop. Let us look at an example to illustrate the difference. Utilizing the Hindu caste once more, the phenomenologist would be interested in describing what the four castes, Brahmins (priestly class), Kshatriyas (warrior or noble class), Vaisyas (mercantile class), and Shudras (servant class), mean to the people of India. From the Hindu perspective the castes have a divine origin. Purusha, representing cosmic man, divided himself up into four parts: his head became the Brahmins, from his arms developed the Kshatriyas, his thighs made up the Vaishyas, and his feet constituted the Shudras. The sociologists, on the other hand, would look for social/human origins to explain how the social distinctions developed. Pulling from historical evidence, some sociologists and historians of religion surmise that the invading Aryans brought the caste system to India over four thousand years ago perhaps as a means to subjugate the indigenous people of India, who were most likely placed in the shudra caste. The term for caste is *varna* which means color. The caste system then may have been a system of color with the indigenous people of darker skin placed in the lowest social position.

Some contemporary sociologists, such as Robin Gill, have suggested that sociology of religion is not simply a value-free science following a purely descriptive model, but it also seems to entail, or at least should, prognosis or a prescription [4]. Following this line of thinking, Rodrick Martain reminds us that the founding fathers of this field--Durkheim, Weber, and Marx--combined the scientific method with philosophical humanitarian concerns or moral considerations, namely, the corrosive effects of the industrial development on the individual and society at large [5]. Many, therefore, argue for an integration of reduction, unmasking ideologies, and humanism, highlighting normative values, since the radical split between the two is not only unnecessary but, in fact, can be detrimental. Society needs to be humanized, they say, and sociology can help bring this about. Thus, the sociologists would not only point out how certain ideas developed but also take a step further by analyzing its positive or negative effects on society and perhaps the direction society should go. For instance, in the case of the caste system, the sociologist would be expected to analyze whether or not these social stratifications (and finger slicing) were morally justifiable. Whether sociologists should serve as humanitarians is still debated today.

Another and more recent discussion within Religious Studies is whether Transpersonal Psychology can offer a new insight to the study of religion. Drawing from Piaget, Kohlberg, Habermas, and Eastern teachers, Ken Wilber, a transpersonal psychologist, contends that for a more accurate and fair analysis of religion we need to incorporate what he calls developmental structuralism [6]. Instead of throwing all religions into the same soup, this approach attempts to discriminate between the different developmental-evolutionary stages of religions, including the prerational, the rational, and the transrational. While a prerational religion promotes egocentricism, mythic mindedness, and conformity of belief and action, a rational religion supports individualism and does not fear science, skepticism, and doubt, and a transrational religion, which incorporates the rational but transcends it, is interested in transformation of consciousness to a higher spiritual-psychological level. The difference between Jim Jones' group and a Zen Buddhist one is obvious to most of us today but to the untutored eye many prerational religions without the cyanide connection may be falsely placed at the same level as transrational religions. However, failing to recognize hierarchical differences is a grave mistake in Religious Studies, says Wilber. Without refined discrimination, those with a pejorative view of religion tend to throw out all religions at once, whereas those with a positive view of religion tend to see all religions as legitimate and authentic. But a critical evaluation of religion, which includes a vertical assessment of the group's developmental level, can remedy this. Thus, according to Wilber sociology of religion needs the methodological tools Transpersonal Psychology has to offer.

Wilberian Developmental Stages of Religion

Prerational: Magical and mythic understanding; group belongingness; conformity; lack of skepticism and doubt; literalistic

Rational: A willingness to doubt and to change one's mind in light of evidence; individual thought; a scientific approach; non-literalistic

Transrational: Sensitivity to higher realms of spirituality; mystical approach with certain techniques such as meditation promoted; rational mind not denied

Dick Anthony in *Spiritual Choices* supports Wilber's thesis, petitioning scholars to distinguish between helpful and harmful groups [7]. Problematic groups usually fall in the prerational, unilevel (literalistic), dualistic (the world is seen as real and God is apart from it), charismatic (personal relationship is necessary with a leader for spiritual growth) category. Less problematic groups, on the other hand, are more multilevel (mystical realms are acknowledge and spiritual growth is a lengthy process), technical (focus is on techniques like meditation) and monistic (a sense of oneness is emphasized). The bottom line here is that scholars are beginning to move away from the purely descriptive approach to one of adjudication. I suspect that transpersonal psychology will have an even greater effect in the future, as scholars begin to realize the import of evaluating the psycho-social level of religions.

A Complete Methodology

Phenomenology: Objectively describing religious phenomena; induction.

Sociology of Religion: Understanding the social origins of religion; reductionism.

Transpersonal Psychology: Assessing the developmental stage of the religion.

Overall, perhaps the best method to study religion is a combination of phenomenology, sociology of religion and transpersonal psychology. Step one, of course, is to objectively describe religious phenomena. Step two would be to critically analyze the data, placing it in a social context and understanding its origins, however human they may be. And, finally, step three is to assess the religion's developmental stage, discriminating among mythic, rational and mystical traditions. What we then have is a balanced approach to study religion, one that takes into consideration 19th century reductionism, 20th century hermeneutics, and 21st century transpersonal studies.

NOTES

1.   See Karl Mannheim's article in Robin Gill's *Theology and Sociology: A Reader* (London: Geoffrey Chapman, 1987).

2.   See Peter Berger's *The Heretical Imperative: Contemporary Possibilities of Religious Affiliation* (Garden City: Anchor Press, 1979).

3.   The core of the scientific method is the utilization of Occam's razor—shaving away "unnecessary, hypothetical entities" and opting for a falsifiable and simpler explanation.

4.   See Robin Gill's *Theology and Sociology: A Reader* (London: Geoffrey Chapman, 1987).

5.   Ibid.

6.   See Ken Wilber's *Sociable God: Toward a New Understanding of Religion* (Boulder: Shambhala, 1984).

7.   See Dick Anthony's *Spiritual Choices: The Problems of Recognizing Authentic Paths to Inner Transformation* (New York: Paragon House, 1987).

What is the Social Function of Religion?

Religion, it seems, entails much more than its manifest or obvious function (from the devotee's perspective this would generally be spiritual liberation); there is also the latent or hidden function that concerns the overall social purpose of religion (what religion accomplishes for society to work properly.) In evaluating the latent function religion is placed in a social context and understood, at least in part, as a human construct. Thus, instead of thinking of religion in theological terms, religion is viewed in a more human light. The social function of religion is generally a hot topic in Religious Studies and so I thought it important to dedicate a chapter to it. Here we will explore the ideas of four prominent sociologists of religion, Simmel, Wilson, Weber, Juergensmeyer, to better comprehend the functionalist stance. A summary of their main text(s) will be given and when appropriate criticism offered.

Georg Simmel

According to Georg Simmel, a sociologist of religion from the continental German tradition, humans are by nature religious. The three components that draw forth humans' religious spirit are: nature, fate and society. Religious feelings of piety, humility and grandeur are invoked as one experiences the powerful forces of the natural world. Also, religiosity is aroused when one embarks on an existential quest for the meaning of life, as one wonders if free will or determinism plays the lead role. The greatest source of religion, however, comes from social relations. Living in a community with others requires a certain cohesiveness that only religion offers.

In *Sociology of Religion* Simmel's main thesis is that religion allows for society to function properly. Without religion, says Simmel, society would not exist, since religion serves as the integrative source for it. His concern is not with the ontological status of religion but the function of religion for social groups. One of the most important roles for religion in society is the construction of religious laws, which, if followed, guarantee some sense of order to the world. For instance, prohibitions like not committing adultery or not killing your neighbor are classified as divine commandments. The proper relations of humans becomes absolutized and projected to the realm of the transcendental, and, consequently, given great importance. Thus, by correlating social obligations with religious ones social norms are regulated.

Aside from implementing restrictive sanctions, religion has the power to create a strong sense of group cohesiveness. Religious rituals such as pilgrimages and festivals represent times of peace when the social hierarchies that separate individuals are lifted. Strong unity is also a product of religious communities, like monasteries, where specific duties are assigned for a common good. This division of labor ensures a dependence on each other and a realization of the importance of the part working for the whole. Under such religious auspices, an innate "love impulse," asserts Simmel, surfaces. Acts of altruism in the name of religion and feelings of brotherhood promote a tightly knit society. In Christianity, this transcendental unity is sometimes referred to as the "Body of Christ" or "The City of God," a state of existence absent of conflict and competition. An outgrowth of the love for fellow humans is love for a projected super-structure--a god. The concept of god plays an essential role in the formation of society. The deity for the group is the ideal projection of the social forces at play. In other words, god personifies the necessary ingredients for group solidarity. It is generally viewed as a loving, just being who wants its people to live peacefully together by following a certain set of pre-ordained rules. Faith in a god is often, then, a great benefit to society. When one believes in a god, it may instill a strong sense of confidence in the future. As long as their god exists, so does the community. And knowing that the group will survive in time perhaps gives greater incentive to work hard at constructing a properly functioning society.

Interestingly, Simmel contends that the god of the group reflects the actual social structure of the group. For instance, when the Jewish community was a singular tribe Yahweh was viewed as a father-like figure who took care of his children. However, when the community grew into an association of several tribes the image of the god stepped out of its narrow confines and was transformed into a more powerful king-like figure who ruled the nation. Thus, the god changes according to the group's dynamics, creating new realities for those with different organizational needs. But the social function of the god does not alter: its primary purpose is group unity. Following Simmel's argument, one could ostensibly predict a community's god (whether it is pantheistic, panentheistic, henotheistic, transtheistic, etc.) by simply observing its social organization.

Simmel, unlike theologians, attempts to ground religion in material culture. As a social "scientist," he opts for simpler, more natural explanations to religion by relating it to possible observable data. His objective is not to de-value religion; rather, he points out the necessity of it. Moreover, he argues that the feelings invoked by religion have their own depth and sincerity, portraying the inner activity of the human psyche.

There are a few problems with Simmel's analysis, however, that should be pointed out. First of all, his definition of religion relies too much on a Judeo-Christian understanding. He implies that religion must have two essential components: 1) belief in a god; and 2) an innerworldly attitude, that is, a drive to promote a prosperous earthly community. Because of his narrow definition, he claims that Buddhism, which has no godhead and does not focus on building strong social ties, is not a religion but a "philosophy." (In Buddhism salvation is possible through the individual's own efforts.) But according to Ninian Smart's more inclusive description of religion, Buddhism indeed can be classified as a religious tradition. Smart defines religion as a "seven-dimensional organism" consisting of: rituals, myths, doctrines, ethics, social institutions, religious material, and religious experiences. This definition of religion seems to correct for any possible Judeo-Christian bias.

Another criticism of Simmel might be his insistence on the social disposition of human beings. In philosophy there has been a long going debate over the nature of humans. John Locke, for instance, argues that humans are basically good creatures, while Thomas Hobbes posits that they are innately asocial. Simmel's argument rests on Locke's position but he offers no evidence at all to support this. His "love impulse" idea may just as easily be replaced with "narcissistic drive," and this would throw his whole theory off.

Moreover, Simmel seems to confuse his role as a social scientist with that of a mystic when he says that true salvation is self-realization, awareness of one's inner most being. Scholars, however, must constantly be on the guard to be objective and impartial and refrain from making such statements in their work.

And, finally, while Simmel tries to ground religion in the world, he really fails to do this because he offers no ethnographic data; rather, he simply "theorizes" about the role in religion. Certainly, hypotheses may precede data collecting, but to adequately validate a claim necessary research must be cited. Specifically, it would be fascinating to see how the image of a god reflects each group's social organization.

Overall, though, Georg Simmel's work deserves a great deal of recognition. His insistence that religion has sociological roots was groundbreaking during the late nineteenth century and has led the way for other sociologists in this area.

Bryan Wilson

In *Religion in Sociological Perspective*, Bryan Wilson takes a strong functionalist stance. His concern is not with the ontology of religion but its social benefits. The manifest, or obvious, function of religion to humans is that it gives a sense of hope, an idea of salvation of some kind. However, religion's latent, or hidden function, claims Wilson, serves an even greater purpose-- social cohesion. In a similar vein with Durkheim, Wilson sees religion as indispensable for a properly functioning society. In a traditional religious society an exhortation to "do the will of God" promotes civic virtue and obligation. While not everyone abides by the moral rules, sanctions recognized by society help to defer actions detrimental to the group. Thus, religion provides the prescriptive moral norms of society; it creates a motive to do good and thus maintains social control.

Besides establishing the overarching values of society religion provides legitimacy to social and political activities, like wars, by declaring them in the "name of God." Religion also creates social unity by giving one a sense of identity as being a part of a group with shared ideas and a sacred history. Usually a myth of origins defining a people's special relations with God is perpetuated. Additionally, religion, through art, dance, and ritual, provides emotional expression essential to human beings. And, finally, as Charles Glock argues, religion helps to console the deprived and hence prevent social rebellion.

However, in the contemporary Western world, traditional religion has become a mere shadow, a result of both pluralism and secularism. Pluralism has played a decisive role in lessening traditional religion by presenting alternative ideologies and promoting choice (the "heretical imperative). For many this means choosing no religious affiliation or at least reducing absolute truths to relativistic claims. Secularism also tremendously affects the impact of traditional religion in society; instead of turning to supernatural help, humans look to the service of science and technology. Yet, without religion playing its essential role, Wilson asserts, society as we know it may become unlivable, devoid of goodwill, community and trust. In place of altruism, hedonism and permissive laissez-faire morality may be the norm. Several signs point to a societal breakdown, asserts Wilson; for instance, he notes the rise of violence in the cities, high suicide and divorce rates, a loss of a sense of community and interpersonal care, disrespect for the elderly, the heavy use of pornography, and an increase in addictions to drugs and gambling. This moral deterioration can clearly be blamed, Wilson says, on the decline of traditional religion.

Wilson admittedly states that his analysis of religion applies specifically to the West and not so much to the East. In Eastern traditions diversity is built into the religious system, allowing for greater appreciation for alternative morals, beliefs and rituals. There is not one Godhead and one set of moral codes but many. Therefore, Wilson argues that in the East a societal breakdown may be avoided altogether since social control is somewhat muted there. However, Wilson claims that this is not the case in the West. Here one finds an exclusive, non-tolerant tradition--Judeo-Christianity--that demands allegiance to an all-powerful God who imposes a rigid set of morals. Humans by nature are deemed sinful and so need rules to help control them. In the Western context, religion plays such a central role in establishing social control that with religion's decline social degeneration is inevitable.

Thus, according to Wilson, without traditional religion in Western society the future looks extremely grim. In fact, he goes as far as to say that without it Western society cannot be fully humane. Of course, there are some benefits to a rationalized society, namely more tolerance and impartiality, but, remarks Wilson, the losses clearly outweigh the gains.

Other agencies, like guild organizations, may attempt to fulfill the role of religion in society, but they do not adequately induce religious sentiment of commitment and concern for others. Wilson argues that the only answer is to revive religion.

An attempt to do this has occurred in the West with the rise of new religious movements, which generally offer the benefits of a tightly knit moral community. However, new religious movements in the West are less concerned with transforming wider society and instead focus their energies on their own group. Hence, the impact of these small, exclusive sects is at best marginal. And Wilson points out that new religious movements, which originally manifest in reaction against secularization, inevitably become more secularized as they attempt to legitimize their position in the rational world. What starts out as an antimodernist group often becomes later a vehicle of secularization itself.

Certainly, Wilson's functionalist stance is fairly reasonable; there are many social benefits from religion, such as creating a sense of social bonding. But upon closer examination of his analysis several problems become apparent. First of all, Wilson seems to ignore contradictory evidence that suggests interpersonal relations in the modern Western world have in many ways improved. Pluralism has exposed people to a variety of alternative cultures and perspectives and the final result may be less prejudice. Tolerance and impartiality are no small feats. Wilson seems to downplay these too much.

Secondly, reviewing history one sees that order was often missing from the social fabric and religion in many cases contributed to this. For instance, in Christianity, considered the moral backbone of the West, numerous decapitations and burnings of so-called heretics were condoned in the name of faith. Indeed, the world appears to have come a long way from the savageries of witch-hunts. Wilson apparently forgets this and assume that earlier times were like the "Donna Reed days" when "gosh-darn-it" was the extent of profanity.

Another problem with Wilson is his apparent anti-science stance. This seems ironic since he introduces his book claiming to follow the scientific method. Yet, in this same piece, he condemns science as de-mystifying and alienating, contributing to the downfall of present day society. However, Wilson fails to realize that science does not necessarily destroy mystery but in many cases reveals it. As Albert Einstein states, "The most beautiful experience we can have is the mysterious. It is the fundamental emotion that stands at the cradle of true art and true science."[From the WORLD AS I SEE IT, 1934] Also, Wilson's claim that science renders the individual in a hopeless state of alienation can be called into question. On the contrary, science can actually induce a feeling of connectedness with nature and the world. Overall, scientific knowledge has taken us quite far, not just into a world of cold machines, but into a world where diseases can be cured and pain stopped. Looking at the cup half empty here, as Wilson does, is perhaps the wrong approach.

Moreover, Wilson's suggestion to return to traditional thinking is ridiculous in the midst of scientific discoveries. Does he still want us to believe that Adam and Eve were historical beings existing 10,000 years ago all for the sake of social cohesion? The mythological world traditional religion endorsed has lost credibility, and a new sacred history, one built on scientific evidence, has won the consensus. Will this new orientation lead to the downfall of the Western world? Of course, from the Judeo- Christian perspective (and Wilson's as well) the answer is yes, since human nature is seen as sinful and in need of very strict moral laws by a binding religious system to keep it in line. However, one can certainly challenge this, as do secular humanists like Paul Kurtz, and describe humans as innately good requiring no religious incentive to be moral. In fact, without traditional religion society may be better off, because human worth will be perhaps more greatly valued.

But how then does one explain the increase in violence witnessed today? Perhaps it is a typical pattern of disillusionment and acted-out frustration that occurs whenever society is experiencing a transition from one paradigm to another--in this case from traditional religion to secularism. In time, when the new worldview (or, if you will, "religion," using Paul Tillich's definition of it) eventually takes hold, tensions are lessened and society re-bonded under a new vision. One can point to several examples in history that indicate this pattern: for instance, there was much documented violence during the rise of Islam and even the beginnings of the Reformation.

Thus, Wilson's claim that today's decline in traditional religion has led to an unprecedented deterioration of society is questionable. If instead there is a cyclical process of decline and rebirth occurring in society throughout history, then the future may not be as forbidding as Wilson predicts. Religion, defined here as one's "ultimate concern," may still fulfill its role creating social cohesion, but perhaps in a new form--secularism.

Max Weber

In his seminal work *The Protestant Ethic and the Spirit of Capitalism,* Max Weber argues that religious ideology can in itself act as an instrument for social change. This is naturally in contrast with Karl Marx, who felt that social position determines ideology. Weber, while not necessarily disputing Marx's point, contends that ideas can affect the course of how people interact. And to buttress this point Weber looks to religion and how religious ideas dovetail with other social productions into altering human beings' overall socio-economic stance.

In a magnificent case study Weber examines how Protestantism played a major role in initiating modern capitalism. He began his study when he noticed that business leaders and owners of capital were predominately Protestant and thus subscribed to a particular *ethos* that Weber realized was essential for capitalism.

To begin with, Protestantism rejected the outer worldly asceticism of the Catholic Church and instead embraced a different approach to the world--inner worldly asceticism. One was not to shriek one's duties in the world retiring to monastic servitude as the Catholics suggested, but actively engage in the world dedicating all work to the glory of God.

According to Weber, inner worldly asceticism is a very powerful force for social change and greatly contributed to the spirit of capitalism that swept through Europe and North America. This form of asceticism is captured most consistently in Calvinism, which clearly advanced the concept of a divine "calling"--a duty to glorify God through hard work and self-control. Unlike traditional Catholicism, God was not to be found simply in a religious retreat but in all areas on life, including the market place.

For the first time in Christianity the pursuit of wealth was welcomed and sanctified. Profit itself was seen as a sign of God's stewardship. Yet, this pursuit was not untamed. The new ethos entailed not only industry (making money) but sober-mind and frugality (investing one's money back into the business itself). Hence, the capitalists generally did not live a life of luxury, believing that the greatest return was for those who postpone their enjoyment.

This is clearly an ascetic view, since it involves a very defined sense of the future, while thinking of the present as something temporary and also as something to transcend. If this sense of time, this sense of present asceticism is absent, then it is more difficult for an economic system like capitalism to develop. Why? Because it takes a certain kind of approach to the world in order to understand what Benjamin Franklin meant when he said a "penny saved is a penny earned." The idea of saving is essentially present moment denying; yet, why deny this present moment if it is all that there is? But, to Weber's credit, he saw that to a Protestant there is in fact more to life than the present moment--there is, to be certain, a future--and, as Christianity posits, a glorious future at that.

As for the poor laborers themselves, they were viewed as highly pleasing to God if they remained faithful workers even at low wages. This resulted in an essential element of capitalism--legalized exploitation. Predictably, few workers rebelled since any attitude or outlook that might undermine the system was viewed as extremely sinful.

All things considered, little wonder, therefore, that capitalism thrives in those countries where a Protestant "ethic" flourishes. It is this philosophical underpinning, so to say, which contributes to the success of this world-postponing system. Marx may have been correct in identifying how economic factors determine ideology, but Weber clearly demonstrates that this is only part of the picture. As we see, religious influences have their own force, creating conditions favorable to a new economic civilization.

Weber's study is one of only a handful of sociological studies that can be termed a classic. It is a classic precisely because it has done what most sociological studies have not: passed the test of time and still been useful some eight decades after its initial publication. What makes the study so useful is that it combines theory with an empirical case. In other words, it does what every good scientific endeavor should: explain disparate data by a simpler theory, while at the same time being open to verification or to falsification. As such, it serves as a model of the interactionist approach (suggesting a mutual interaction between ideas and behavior) for many future sociological studies.

Mark Juergensmeyer

Mark Juergensmeyer in *Religion as Social Vision* agrees with Weber that one of the more successful ways to promote social change is through religious movements. Oppressed groups who want to restructure society may turn to religion as a vehicle for social improvement, since, unlike purely political movements, religious ones seem to have a stronger sense of cohesion--a feeling of communitas--which gives strength to their fight. A new social vision, described as a religious utopia, becomes the group's foci. In a case study, Juergensmeyer investigates the Untouchables of India to demonstrate how such a "political religion" works.

The Untouchables of India face intense discrimination, endorsed by the Hindu religion itself. According to the Hindu scriptures, the Vedas, the caste system was divinely ordained and the Untouchables are at the bottom of it. They are ranked so low in society they are sometimes referred to as Outcastes-- outside of the four varnas or castes. While living simple lives as street sweepers, leather workers, beggars and landless laborers, the Untouchables, viewed as impure, face tremendous oppression. Not only are they forbidden to eat with the other higher castes, there are strict rules against mingling with them as well. In the Hindu code of ethics, *The Laws of Manu*, it explains that there is no opportunity to improve one's position since one's caste is hereditary (based on the laws of karma). It continues to add that one should gracefully accept one's social position and hope for a higher caste rank in the next life.

There have been some attempts in the twentieth century, however, to change the plight of the Untouchables. For instance, Gandhi tried to raise the status of the Untouchables by referring to them as "Harijan," translated as the "children of God," and by incorporating them as equals into the Hindu fold. Yet, many Untouchables resented Gandhi's effort, considering it implicitly patronizing. Rather than identify with the Hindus, their oppressors, a large number of Untouchables sought separation from them. New religious movements sprang up in the early 1900's with this in mind.

Since their oppression stems from Hindu religious concepts, by cleverly embracing a religion of their own the Untouchables turned Hinduism on its head and offered alternative interpretations and a new social vision. In other words, they fought religion with religion. The Untouchables sometimes even utilized traditional Hindu religious symbols, albeit with a new twist, as a way to couch political and social ambitions in a familiar religious language and thus to challenge normative order.

The Ad Dharm movement, founded by Mangoo Ram in the 1920's, is a classic example of an "Untouchable religion." Its goal was liberation for the Untouchables and it campaigned for this through religious mythology. Religious myths, such as a myth of divine origin as "a special people of God" who have somehow fallen from their esteemed position at the hands of oppressors, are evoked to give the group identity and instill a sense of purpose--a drive to regain a lost status. Adherents claimed that their religion existed from time immemorial and that they were the original people of India. When Aryans (Indo-Europeans) invaded India, asserted the Ad Dharm leaders, they implemented the caste system to justify subjugating the indigenous people. According to Mangoo Ram, the objective of the Ad Dharm was to call the non-Aryan people back to their heritage. While the Aryan invasion is historically grounded, the Ad Dharm movement certainly flavored the account. In an attempt to establish their superiority over the upper classes, the Untouchables identified with the original people of India some 4,500 years ago; however, an uninterrupted ancestral link is uncertain.

The Ad Dharm tradition was not looking for equality in the Hindu world but mainly separation from it. It rejected the Arya Samaj movement ("Society of Aryans"), which sought to establish a new Hinduism for the middle class and to accept as equal women and the lower classes; instead, the Untouchables fought for their own sense of cultural identity.

Signs of a separate quam (religious community) became visible under the leadership of Mangoo Ram. To set themselves apart from other religions, the Untouchables developed their own greeting. They also, in rebellion, wore the color red, sacred in Hinduism and usually prohibited for the Untouchables. As solidarity grew, political-religious rallies become even more vibrant. Heroes, usually lower caste gurus like Ravi Das, were venerated at the meetings. Moreover, as with most religious traditions, the Ad Dharm had its own religious writings, which highlighted moral requirements and presented humanitarian objectives clothed in religious ideology.

Officially, the Ad Dharm made its mark as a distinct group during the 1931 census. Their high numbers posed a serious threat to other religious groups who were competing for legislative seats and representation. Numbers translated as electoral power, and this bargaining leverage could be their ticket out of bondage. While many Untouchables feared identification with the Ad Dharm because of local harassment and widespread intimidation, the movement still pulled in a significant percentage. Mangoo Ram claimed this as their first real victory in the socio-political arena.

What helped their cause was the positive relationship the Ad Dharm had with the ruling British government. The government had a vested interest in promoting the Ad Dharm, since this movement was not a Hindu or Sikh anti-British nationalistic organization. If the huge number of Untouchables in India were diverted from joining the anti-British nationalist cause and instead encouraged to have their own movement the British government would certainly feel less threatened. On the other side, the motivation of the Ad Dharm to support the British government is clear: it in turn would receive government benefits such as education for children and independence from the upper classes, such as recognition as a distinct group from the Hindus in the 1931 census. The relationship was, therefore, a symbiotic one. With the British support, the Ad Dharm became a political force.

However, the Ad Dharm took a turn for the worst in the late 1930's when it became too political and lost its religious vision. With its gained electoral strength, politics seemed to become its sole emphasis. Leaders were no longer religious figures fighting for the freedom of the downtrodden, but politicians with personal ambitions and secular interests. They were now "outsiders" who had less concern at the local level and were alienated from their constituency. Hence, when the Ad Dharm abandoned religion for politics it lost its unifying symbols and thus its strength. Three decades went by before the Ad Dharm movement realized its mistake. Yet, in the 1970's Mangoo Ram Jaspal advocated a "new" Ad Dharm--a religious one--which is growing significantly today.

Juergensmeyer's investigation of the Untouchables of India clearly illustrates how religion can serve as a source for social improvement. In many ways his analysis challenges Karl Marx's ideas of religion. According to Marx, religion, like a numbing "opium," dulls the pain of oppression and inhibits social rebellion by offering false hopes of a heavenly future (or, in the case of India, a higher caste position). Marx's theory may indeed

54

explain the persistence of the caste system in India through the millennia but in the last one hundred years we witness a turn of events: an onset of new religious movements whose objective is to liberate the lower classes. Thus, instead of perpetuating oppression, religion can possibly serve to emancipate.

Interestingly, when Marxists entered India with ideals of equality and plans to recruit, they were disappointed (and somewhat embarrassed) when the Untouchables showed no interest in their secular philosophy. Certainly, the Outcastes were ripe for recruitment but they needed religion as the instrument for social change. Religion supplied necessary ingredients such as hope for the future and a sense of importance.

Conclusion: The Future of Religion

Some protest reference to God in the Pledge of Allegiance to the Flag and on the dollar bill. Others challenge clubs like the Boy Scouts for not admitting atheists into the organization. Intellectuals on campus's worldwide proudly profess their emancipation from religious ideology. As there is no doubt that secularism has increased in our society and in the world at large, the question surfaces: in the future should we expect religion totally to wane? Well, unlike Wilson, I will argue that religion due to its dynamic and resilient nature will be around for a long, long time.

To begin with, it is important to understand that religion is never static but is constantly changing and evolving. What was once a conservative religion at odds with society eventually accommodates itself and becomes more moderate to a liberal version. But this is only half of the process, asserts H. Richard Niebuhr. As a conservative religion adapts from high tension with society to low, becoming an established movement, schisms or sects develop with the objective to return to traditional ways and to the supposedly "correct" interpretations. What we have is a never-ending cycle: conservative religions become moderate, then liberal; liberal religions become secular; and sects become conservative church movements to start the whole process over again [1].

Three Types of Religious Groups

Established Religion: Mainstream religion; low tension with society; it once was a sect or a cult that proved successful as it adapted itself to social needs and survived

Sect: A breakaway or schism group from an established religion; high tension with society; there is usually an attempt to restore what is viewed as the "original teachings"

Cult: A new religious movement; high tension with society; religious group may be totally new or simply new to a particular society (e.g., Buddhism on American soil)

What this means for the future of religion is significant: religion will endure. Of course, it seems that in our day and age with the advancement of science and the secularization of society religion will not be able to hold its ground. But this is indeed a misunderstanding of the whole dynamic process of religion. All religious economies have experienced secularization of some form or another, and it is this very secularization that allows for new religious trends to spring forth. In a sense, secularization is the fuel of religion; it stimulates religious innovation.

In this final chapter we will examine evidence that religion is not approaching its death but being reinvigorated in new, fascinating forms. Our interest will be on the rise of fundamentalism, the onslaught of cults, and the impact of the baby boomer generation on the religious scene.

Religious Trends in America

Fundamentalist Groups on the increase Cults on the increase

Secularism on the increase

Liberal Protestantism on the decline

Established Religions being transformed by the baby boomer generation

The Rise of Fundamentalism

In modern America religious extremism, sometimes referred to as orthodoxy, is growing. The secularization thesis as argued by Peter Berger, which suggests that in the face of secularism religion will eventually lose its vitality, is being challenged. Some have even argued that America is in for a "Third Great Awakening" as orthodox religions, once marginal, are becoming mainstream.

The driving force behind orthodoxy is modernity. Orthodox religions promote very conservative theologies, morals and worldly dispositions in an attempt to fortress themselves against secular society. Many are attracted to conservatism in reaction to a rapidly changing world, where prayer is banned in public schools, abortion and homosexuality are more accepted, and many women demand equal rights. The taken-for-granted sense of reality that existed prior to the sixties exists no more and this is frightening for some. Common are modern life dilemmas, such as isolation, rootlessness and confusion about gender roles. Since it offers a strong sense of belonging and clear guidelines on how to live one's life, many turn to an orthodox religious community as an antidote to the ills of society. Such a community usually advocates a "return to traditional ways" and the re-establishment of an ordered and predictable world.

An example of an attempt to return to tradition is the promotion of the "traditional family model," with the male as the breadwinner and head of the home, and the woman as submissive and childbearing. According to Wade Clark Roof in American Mainline Religion, the "traditional family model" plays a decisive role in affecting the growth of orthodox religions, since such a model contributes to high birth rates and thus an increase in followers. (On the other hand, Liberal Protestantism, which de-emphasizes the "traditional family model," is experiencing a decrease in the number of religious practitioners.)

However, the argument that one can "return to tradition," that there is direct continuity with the past, is a bit fallacious. Religions are constantly being reconstituted in reaction to cultural forces, and so "pure" orthodoxy is not really possible. Many conservative religious ideas are not ancient but are in fact a mesh of new and old religious concepts. Nonetheless, the idea of "returning to tradition" is for many very comforting and may be a coping strategy in the midst of an overwhelming modern world of change.

Perhaps no other religion has had to confront the changes of modernity as Christianity has. In defense against new intellectual movements (such as evolution) and alternative religions brought by immigrants a strong conservative Christian movement began in sectarian fervor in the late nineteenth century. Attempting to purge "heresy," several Christian conferences were held and numerous newspapers published advocating a "return" to Christian ways of living. This movement, though, was split in the 1940's due to ideological differences, resulting in two main camps: The American Council of Christian Churches (supported by ultra-conservative Fundamentalists) and The National Association of Evangelicals (supported by somewhat less extreme, although still orthodox, Christians known as Evangelicals).

Nancy Ammerman in *Bible Believers: Fundamentalists in the Modern World* describes Fundamentalism as a militant anti-modern organization of independent churches that allows absolutely no room for compromise. Sharp lines are drawn clearly demarcating the "true bible believers" (the "saved") from all the others denominations and faiths. Some of their greatest battles are fought against other Christian branches, which offer an alternative interpretation to Christianity and thus are some-times viewed as even more threatening than non-Christian religions, including atheism. One of Fundamentalists' defining characteristics is their insistence on biblical literalism. The bible is viewed as neither subjective nor symbolic but an inerrant book of objective truth including ultimate answers to everything, even in the areas of science and history. Any form of biblical criticism is vehemently rejected. Moreover, most Fundamentalists exercise rigid moral standards, prohibiting drinking alcohol, dancing, and, in many cases, watching television. The "outside" secular world is often denounced as Satanic, and thick, insulating walls are built.

Evangelicals are also warriors against modernity, promoting a return to "old-time" religion. However, unlike the Fundamentalists, they are generally not as extremist in their position, attempting to at least cooperate with other Christian denominations. In some sense, then, Evangelicalism is a softer version than Fundamentalism. And this "softening" trend is even becoming more pronounced in the younger, more educated Evangelicals. James Davidson Hunter in *Evangelicalism: The Coming Generation* points out that the new generation has been exposed to more education and, consequently, is a lot more tolerant toward other faiths and life styles than the past generation. Describing Evangelicals as anti-intellectual bigots, says Hunter, is a misnomer. Other forms of accommodating to modernity include a greater acceptance of biblical contextualism and a rejection of religious exclusiveness. While orthodoxy may not be eroding for the Evangelicals, it certainly is being redefined here. Accommodation generally occurs because for the sect to be successful and not die out it must gather a significant following, and one way to accomplish this is to appeal to mainstream society. What initially started out as a sectarian resistance movement begins to slowly compromise more and more with modern thinking; although in comparison to the secular world it is still very conservative.

Classic Orthodox Groups

Fundamentalism: An extreme conservative movement of Christianity that promotes biblical literalism, a return to the traditional family model, rigid moral standards; the group developed as a reaction to secularism and modernity

Evangelicalism: A conservative branch of Christianity, though less strict than the fundamentalist version; for instance, biblical contextualism is gaining some acceptance

Orthodox Judaism: This branch of Judaism resembles Fundamentalist Christians in its conservative position; biblical literalism and religious exclusiveness are again highlighted

Religious extremism is also gaining ground in Judaism. Lynn Davidman's ethnographic study, *Tradition in a Rootless World*, indicates that many Jewish Americans today are attracted to orthodoxy because they are discontent with contemporary culture. But, as in orthodox Christianity, there are different responses to the secular world, some more extreme than others. Davidman studied two different orthodox communities (Hasidic and Modern Orthodox), in order to compare these responses.

In her research, which focused on women in Judaism, she noticed that younger, less educated women who experienced a serious crises or came from a troubled family background were pulled more toward Hasidic Judaism, a staunchly conservative branch, and those attracted to Modern Orthodoxy were generally professional, older women who were seeking some solitude in an ever changing world. The former group experiences complete resocialization from the modern world and adapts completely new patterns of behavior and interactions, while the latter allows for some reconciliation between traditionalism and modernism and in a sense lives a bi-cultural existence. Seekers, then, seem to be attracted to religious communities that suit their needs.

Yet, while there is a rise of fundamentalism in Christianity and Judaism, it seems improbable that it will become America's new religious center determining American values. First of all, too many divisions occur within the conservative branches, generally between those who permit accommodation and those who fight to retain traditional thinking. And since a greater number of people today attend college, where they are taught tolerance and skepticism, there may develop even further schisms in the future. A national religious revival, a "Third Great Awakening" in America, would probably require greater cohesion than this.

In addition, what works against a "Third Great Awakening" is the intense growth of secularism. Liberal Protestantism, which used to be at the religious center in America, is losing many potential adherents to the secular drift. Prior to contemporary society, many of the educated were attracted to Liberal Protestantism, but now they fit more comfortably into the secularist camp. Also, more and more Liberal Protestants themselves are forsaking their tradition for secularism. The great emphasis on individualism within Liberal Protestantism has allowed for a smooth transition to secular thought. (For some, however, a new climate of freedom--what Roof calls "new voluntarism"--has led to an interest in experiential religion and an overall less involvement in organized religion.)

Hence, in America today, instead of a strong, conservative religious center, there continues to exist a "fragmented middle." Most likely, the religious scene will further divide as people react to modernity in different ways, either accommodating to it to a certain degree or resisting it altogether. The trends of religion, namely the growth of secularism and conservatism and the decline of Liberal Protestantism, will probably persist for some time.

The Cult Phenomenon

How do cults fit into all of this? Cults, unlike sects, are not schisms since they have no connection to a parent religion; rather, cults are completely new movements in a society. They may have been church movements or sects from another culture imported into a new land, such as Mahesh Yogi's Transcendental Meditation brought into America, or may simply be a radically new group manifesting for the first time, such as L. Ron Hubbard's Scientology. Like sects, religious cults are in high tension with social mainstream but are also subject to accommodation and secularization. While cults are not the result of schism, they are vulnerable to it; hence, sects may break off from cults.

Not all cults are religions, however. Some cults deal solely with magic, that is, the manipulation of natural forces for a specific end or reward. On the other hand, religion, as Emile Durkheim points out, offers general compensators relating to the supernatural, such as claims of an afterlife. Religion has a definite advantage over magic: magic is susceptible to disproof if the promises of specific benefits are not actualized, while the claims of religion are non-falsifiable and hence not vulnerable to empirical verification.

Some cults, like Scientology, start off as a magic cult, offering through magical means access to a high mental state called clear-status, entailing perfect memory and genius I.Q. The problem with such claims is that they can be disproved. And in the case of Scientology they were. Consequently, Hubbard began to focus on more general compensators like ideas of reincarnation and admission into a heavenly sphere.

Two Types of Cults

Magic Cults: Groups that deal with manipulating nature and focus on specific rewards; there are no general compensators relating to the supernatural

Religious Cults: New religions that claim to offer supernatural benefits of some kind

The same trend from magic to religion occurred in the Transcendental Meditation movement. Originally, it presented itself as a "science" devoid of the supernatural. The goal was higher awareness through meditation. It became a religion only when it began to offer general compensators such as siddhis, or supernatural powers. It did so right when there was a huge decline in membership, perhaps as an attempt to present a shiny new product when sales were down. Soon after it was ruled in the courts a religion and prevented from entering school classrooms.

Many parents fear that their children will be brainwashed by such cult formations. But the "brainwashing theory" is very inconsistent with this overall analysis of religion. Well-balanced, educated people may be attracted to a cult religion not only because it is novel and exotic, but, like sect or church movements, it allows social bonding and offers general compensators, both of which seem to be basic needs of humans.

Most importantly, we must remember that all religions started at some time or another as a cult or a sect. Conventional religions practiced today are simply those sects or cults that were successful and were able to accommodate to mainstream society and attract a following. Christianity itself began as a cult; it was different enough from Judaism not to be considered a sect. In its early stages it assumed an otherworldly position and experienced high-tension with society, as the Roman persecutions will attest. In its two thousand year history a variety of sects, including the Protestant movements, emerged. And as these movements moved from conservatism to secularism, more cleavages occurred. The result is an ever-growing and changing religious scene. As a missionary movement, Christianity was again of cult status, entering foreign lands with a foreign message.

As we see, cults cannot be blamed on the sixties, as some have tried to do. They are an essential element of the whole process of religion and are found throughout history in all societies. What actually facilitates their growth is secularization. Secularization does not produce an irreligious society, a popular claim among many sociologists, but an unchurched one interested in religious experimentation. It makes sense that cults abound where conventional religion is weak, such as in California. And, predictably, since much of Judaism has been secularized, cults are very popular among Jews. Sects, on the other hand, flourish where conventional religion is strong but has begun to accommodate to the social environment too much for some church members.

Arguably, in the future there will be a continuation of cult formation. As for magic and pseudoscience, it may possibly die out, since science has the advantage of now disproving such claims. But we most likely will never enter into a post-religious era, since religion seems to be a necessary constant in society with its general compensators, secure from scientific evaluation, giving hope and meaning to people's lives.

The Baby Boomer Effect

Who have helped set religious trends in America in the last few decades? Generally, it is the baby boomers (those born between 1946 and 1964). Since there are roughly 76 million baby boomers today, about one third of America, the mindset of this cohort will no doubt permeate the cultural mainstream and have a significant effect on religion and where it is heading in our country. As baby boomers are approaching mid-life to the latter stages of life, for many it is a time of reassessment, deep reflection, and sometimes a change in religious views. Wade Clark Roof, in *A Generation of Seekers*, investigates the repercussions all of this has on America at large.

While there are enormous differences among baby boomers (the rich mosaic includes hippies, yuppies, liberals, new agers, secularists, even fundamentalists), there are also major commonalities that set this generation off as a distinct group. For instance, unlike the earlier generations that tended to unquestioningly accept the institutional tradition handed down to them, baby boomers, asserts Roof, are a "generation of seekers" on a spiritual quest. As a whole, boomers place emphasis on religious experience and, most importantly, on personal choice. They tend to differentiate between "religion" and "spirituality," with a preference for the latter, indicating a more subjective, experiential approach to religion. For some, organized religion is distrusted, viewed as too ritualistic, alienating and rule oriented.

Moreover, for most boomers the concept of God has been altogether transformed. In traditional Judeo-Christianity God is generally viewed as a transcendent being removed from nature. But boomers tend to embrace an Emersonian view of divinity, a holistic view of the world, where God, or the sacred, is part and parcel with nature. Valuing nature or being in harmony with it, through environmental movements like Earth Day, is for many a way to respect God. Several even describe God as Mother, similar to the nurturing image of Mother Earth.

Not only has the image of God changed, the perception of the self has also. Most boomers reject the Calvinistic idea that the self is evil and argue instead that it is good by nature. In fact, many speak of the "divinity" within each self and the importance of introspection and self-realization. The self, therefore, has great potential for growth and healing, the central theme of so many self-improvement books and classes available today (including 12-step programs). Physical exercise, like jogging and hatha yoga, is also encouraged, since the body, working in harmony with the spirit, is now more fully appreciated. This optimistic view of human nature has contributed to the idea of creating a new planetary society, referred to by many as the "new age" to come.

Typical Baby Boomer Characteristics

Interest in self-improvement

Holistic view of the world

A more tolerant attitude

Emersonian view of divinity

Focus on religious experience

Perhaps we can explain the boomers' preoccupation with inner-self development by examining Abraham Maslow's "hierarchy of needs" idea. According to Maslow, once one's economic survival needs are met, there is now time for self-actualization. Since the baby boomer generation is in many ways the most prosperous of any group in history, it can now afford to concentrate on Maslow's final stage.

Many have criticized baby boomers for being narcissistic, but this is unfair, says Roof. The focus on the self is not to be understood as selfishness, but rather a desire for self-awareness. And this is not necessarily antithesis of community. As Joseph Butler argues, self-love and benevolence are two fundamental principles that work together. Recent surveys indicate that most boomers yearn for a sense of community and have a great interest in social justice.

Additionally, boomers tend to be more tolerant of other lifestyles and beliefs than the preceding generations. This is most likely due to the fact that boomers have received more education and hence greater exposure to alternative perspectives, especially in humanities courses. As expected, cultural relativism and religious universalism (the belief that all religions speak a truth) are significantly more popular among boomers than religious absolutism is.

These general traits (privatism, spirituality, holism and relativism) are found throughout the baby boomer generation, whether loyalist, dropout or returnee. Loyalists (about thirty-three percent of boomers) are those who have remained loyal to their family's religion, while dropouts (about forty-two percent of boomers) have left institutional religion, either to embrace alternative religions, most likely what Ernst Troeltsch calls "mystical religion," or perhaps a purely secular approach. Approximately twenty-five percent of boomers fall into the third subculture, returnees. This group is of special interest to sociologists since they have returned to institutional religion and have had a major effect on transforming it. Why they returned can be explained by considering at least three factors: first of all, boomers are entering mid-life and the later stages of life and asking serious questions about life's meaning and religion offers many answers; secondly, many have reared children and wanted to raise their family with some religious background; and, finally, for those experiencing a form of mid-life or later life crises, institutional religions offer support groups and a sense of belonging to a community.

Three Groups of Baby Boomers

Loyalists: Approximately thirty three percent remain loyal to their religious upbringing

Dropouts: Approximately forty two percent drop out of mainstream religion; for this group either alternative religions or secularism are embraced

Returnees: Approximately twenty five percent of baby boomers fit here; returnees change religion from within as they contribute new religious attitudes and trends

What does all of this possibly mean for religion in America? Very simply, religion in America has changed and the baby boomers were in large part responsible for it. Instead of religion disappearing in the modern world, as some have speculated, it simply seems to change forms, taking different expressions for different generations. For the baby boomer generation Western dualism needs to be overcome; for them, the sacred is found in nature and can be personally experienced. Perhaps, as Roof states, only under this new guise could the notion of the sacred continue to exist in the secular world.

Thus, religion's future does not look so grim. Religion may actually be growing as this large group approaches their middle to elder years, reevaluates life, and looks to religion as a source of comfort and community. As conventional religion lost ground to the baby boomers' version, new American religious trends have been set, and, hopefully, as Roof suggests, both a "mature" self-image and more fulfilling religious perspective will continue to flourish.

NOTES

1. See Rodney Stark's and William Bainbridge's *The Future of Religion: Secularization, Revival and Cult Formation* (Berkeley: University of California Press, 1985).

Select Bibliography

Ammerman, Nancy Tatom. *Bible Believers: Fundamentalists in the Modern World*. New Brunswick: Rutgers University Press, 1987.

Bellah, Robert. *Beyond Belief*. New York: Harper & Row, 1970.

Bellah, Robert, et. al. *Habits of the Heart: Individualism and Commitment in American Life*. New York: Harper & Row, 1985.

Berger, Peter. *The Heretical Imperative: Contemporary Possibilities of Religious Affirmation*. Garden City: Anchor Press, 1979.

Berger, Peter. *The Other Side of God: A Polarity In World Religions*. Garden City: Anchor Press/Doubleday, 1981.

Berger, Peter. *The Sacred Canopy: Elements of a Sociological Theory of Religion*. Garden City: Doubleday, 1967.

Davidman, Lynn. *Tradition in a Rootless World: Women Turn to Orthodox Judaism*. Berkeley: University of California Press, 1991.

Durkheim, Emile. *The Elementary Forms of the Religious Life*. Translated from the French by J. W. Swain. London: Allen and Unwin, 1976.

Eliade, Mircea. *Patterns in Comparative Religion*. Translated by Rosemary Sheed. Cleveland: World Publishing Company, 1963.

Eliade, Mircea. *The Sacred and The Profane: The Nature of Religion*. Chicago: University of Chicago Press, 1959.

Gill, Robin. *Theology and Social Structure*. London: Mowbray, 1977.

Gill, Robin. *Theology and Sociology: A Reader*. London: Geoffrey Chapman, 1987.

Hunter, James Davidson. *Evangelicalism: The Coming Generation*. Chicago: The University of Chicago Press, 1987.

Juergensmeyer, Mark. *Religion as Social Vision*. Berkeley: University of California Press, 1980.

Roof, Wade Clark. *American Mainline Religion: Its Changing Shape and Future*. New Brunswick: Rutgers University Press, 1987.

Roof, Wade Clark. *A Generation of Seekers: The Spiritual Journeys of the Baby Boom Generation*. San Francisco: Harper San Francisco, 1993.

Simmel, Georg. *Sociology of Religion*. New York: Arno Press, 1979.

Stark, Rodney and Bainbridge, W. *The Future of Religion: Secularization, Revival and Cult Formation*. Berkeley: University of California Press, 1985.

Wach, Joachim. *Sociology of Religion*. Chicago: University of Chicago Press, 1944.

Weber, Max. *The Protestant Ethic and the Spirit of Capitalism*. Translated by Talcott Parsons. New York: Scribner, 1976.

Weber, Max. *The Religion of India: The Sociology of Hinduism and Buddhism*. Translated by Hans Gerth. New York: Free Press, 1968.

Weber, Max. *The Sociology of Religion*. Translated by Ephrain Fischoff. Boston: Beacon Press, 1963.

Wilber, Ken. *A Sociable God: Toward A New Understanding of Religion*. Boulder: Shambhala, 1984.

Wilber, Ken. *Eye to Eye*. New York: Doubleday, 1983.

Wilson, Bryan. *Religion in Sociological Perspective*. Oxford: Oxford University Press, 1982.

About the Author

Andrea Diem-Lane is a Professor of Philosophy at Mt. San Antonio College. She received her Ph.D. and M.A. in Religious Studies from the University of California, Santa Barbara, where she did her doctoral studies under Professor Ninian Smart. Professor Diem-Lane received a B.A. in Psychology with an emphasis on Brain Research from the University of California, San Diego, where she did pioneering visual cortex research under the tutelage of Dr. V.S. Ramachandran. Dr. Diem-Lane is the author of several books including an interactive textbook on consciousness entitled *The Cerebral Mirage* and an interactive book on the famous Einstein-Bohr debate over the implications of quantum theory entitled *Spooky Physics*. Her most recent book is *Darwin's DNA: An Introduction to Evolutionary Philosophy*.